YES, I CAN (*SÍ, YO PUEDO*)

YES, I CAN (*SÍ, YO PUEDO*)

AN EMPOWERMENT PROGRAM

FOR IMMIGRANT LATINA WOMEN

IN GROUP SETTINGS

The *Yes, I Can (Sí, Yo Puedo) Program Manual for Mental Health Professionals* is an 11-week curriculum designed to provide education on domestic violence, promote self-esteem, prevent domestic violence, and understand healthy relationships within a cultural framework

 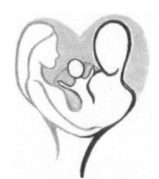  

Catherine Luz Marrs Fuchsel, PhD, LICSW, LCSW, MSW

ASSOCIATE PROFESSOR
ST. CATHERINE UNIVERSITY
ST. PAUL, MINNESOTA

OXFORD
UNIVERSITY PRESS

OXFORD
UNIVERSITY PRESS

Oxford University Press is a department of the University of Oxford. It furthers the University's objective of excellence in research, scholarship, and education by publishing worldwide. Oxford is a registered trade mark of Oxford University Press in the UK and certain other countries.

Published in the United States of America by Oxford University Press
198 Madison Avenue, New York, NY 10016, United States of America.

Library of Congress Cataloging-in-Publication Data
Names: Marrs Fuchsel, Catherine Luz, author.
Title: Yes, I can, (sí, yo puedo) : an empowerment program for immigrant
Latina women in group settings / Catherine Luz Marrs Fuchsel, PhD, LICSW, LCSW, MSW,
Associate Professor, St. Catherine University, St. Paul, Minnesota, U.S.A.
Description: New York, NY : Oxford University Press, [2017] |
"The SYP Program Manual for Mental Health Professionals is an 11-week Curriculum
Designed to Provide Education on Domestic Violence, Promote Self-esteem,
Prevent Domestic Violence, and Understand Healthy Relationships within a
Cultural Framework." | Includes bibliographical references and index.
Identifiers: LCCN 2017013728 (print) | LCCN 2017030051 (ebook) |
ISBN 978-0-19-067283-6 (updf) | ISBN 978-0-19-067284-3 (epub) |
ISBN 978-0-19-067285-0 (Online Component) | ISBN 978-0-19-067282-9 (alk. paper)
Subjects: LCSH: Latin Americans—Services for—United States. | Latin Americans—
Mental health services—United States. | Immigrant women—Services for—United States. |
Social work with immigrants—United States. | Social work with women—United States. |
Social work with Hispanic Americans. | Family violence—Prevention—United States.
Classification: LCC HV3187.A2 (ebook) | LCC HV3187.A2 M37 2017 (print) |
DDC 362.82/9286—dc23
LC record available at https://lccn.loc.gov/2017013728

9 8 7 6 5 4 3 2 1

Printed by WebCom, Inc., Canada

This book is dedicated to all of the immigrant Latina women and Latino families I encountered in my 19-year career as a clinical social worker and social work educator in the United States who made every effort to improve their lives, relationships, and families.

CONTENTS

AUTHOR'S NOTE

The different sections of the *Sí, Yo Puedo* (SYP) program manual were designed to provide an overview of the SYP curriculum and program, background information on domestic violence and immigrant Latina women, a theoretical understanding of group work and group dynamics, and instructions on how to conduct the weekly group format sessions. At the core of the SYP program manual is a step-by-step guide and "how to" book for bilingual graduate-level and licensed Spanish-English mental health professionals. Mental health professionals from different disciplines who work with immigrant Latina women and their families can use the program manual to offer educational and empowerment groups in direct practice settings and different agency contexts.

Often, I received feedback from reviewers that I should expand the SYP curriculum and program to include other groups of women nationally and internationally. This feedback is imperative, and it is a vision I have—to translate the SYP program manual/book into Spanish and write future editions that expand across cultures and are accessible to different groups of women. Reviewers have also suggested making the SYP curriculum and program accessible to generalist social workers with bachelor degrees or mental health professionals in the United States and elsewhere with bachelor-level knowledge. This idea is also very important. Currently, the SYP program manual/book is designed for mental health professionals who are licensed with graduate-level degrees. I am aware that many community-based agencies sometimes cannot hire or contract these types of professionals, or communities simply do not have professionals with graduate educational degrees on a national and international level. For those reasons, a second vision I have is to further expand this idea and to begin a SYP Training and Consultation Institute with licensed, graduate-level mental health professionals who can provide supervision and consultation to professionals with bachelor-level educational degrees who want to use the SYP program manual/book in order to conduct these types of groups among immigrant Latinas. *¡Sí, yo puedo!*

ACKNOWLEDGMENTS

The idea of how to best serve immigrant Latina women experiencing domestic violence began from the findings of my doctoral work. The title of the dissertation was *"For Me that Was the Most Important Thing—The Family": The Meaning of Marriage and Domestic Violence among Immigrant Mexican Women* (Marrs, 2007). I would like to acknowledge and thank the members of the doctoral committee (Dr. Karen Gerdes, Chair, Dr. Elizabeth Segal, and Dr. Sharon Murphy) for their wisdom and expertise in assisting in the formulation of the theoretical domestic violence prevention model and hypotheses. The committee members provided the tools I needed to take an important idea and develop an intervention (i.e., the *Yes, I Can (Sí, Yo Puedo)* [SYP] program manual/book, formerly known as the *Domestic Violence Intervention Model: Curriculum and Program Manual for Social Service Providers*) for a vulnerable group of women living in the United States. Thank you for your support, encouragement, and outstanding mentoring!

For the past 19 years, I have worked with hundreds of immigrant Latina women in direct practice settings in southwestern, midwestern, and eastern coastal cities in the United States. Most women identified as being immigrants (specifically women lacking legal status) from Mexico. I provided counseling services in Spanish as a bilingual licensed independent clinical social worker (LICSW). It is from practice experience and high-quality qualitative research investigations of their lived experiences and stories that the SYP curriculum/program was developed. A limited number of immigrant Latina women (e.g., Mexican women) are not able to access domestic violence intervention settings (e.g., shelters or community-based agencies in urban and rural cities) for various reasons (e.g., fear of deportation and issues related to legal status). Accordingly, I developed the 11-week SYP curriculum/program, a psycho-educational group program for immigrant Latina women who do not have access to domestic violence shelters or domestic violence-related programs in community-based agencies. I thank the women for the courage to share their stories with me and for wanting a better life for themselves and their children, for the courage to try to keep their families intact despite difficult circumstances, and for wanting to have healthy relationships in their homes.

The evaluation of the SYP curriculum/program has been in production for five years (2011–2016). My team and I have conducted eleven groups with a total of 88 participants over a five-year period, collecting qualitative data that has shaped the development of the SYP curriculum/program. I would like to thank the participants and group facilitators who took part and are taking part in the ongoing project. The information they provided on the weekly topics in the program has been very valuable to the development of the SYP curriculum/program. The first evaluation of the SYP curriculum/program (2011–2013) took place at a community-based health clinic in a rural city in Minnesota. I would like to acknowledge the community-based health clinic (i.e., four groups were conducted; $n = 36$). This project would not have been possible without their assistance, collaboration, and backing of the program. The community-based health clinic provided the staff, group setting location, and food and childcare support.

In 2013–2016, four groups were conducted ($n = 32$) at Centro, the largest Latino community-based agency in the Minneapolis/St. Paul metropolitan area. Centro provides educational services and strengthens families by helping them maintain their Latino cultural values and beliefs. In addition to the collection of weekly qualitative data on the topics, pre- and posttest surveys were administered to participants at the initial intake meeting and upon completion of the program. Pre- and posttest survey questions assessed for change in knowledge of domestic violence and healthy relationships and self-esteem. I would like to thank Roxana Linares, executive director at Centro, for believing in the program and providing the group facilitators, support staff, location space, childcare, food, and administrative support. Because of her commitment to the research project, survey data continues to be collected and analyzed to assess for change among the participants. I would also like to thank Ana Abugattas and Diana Loaiza Tangarife, the group facilitators, for working above and beyond in the evaluation and administering of the program. Finally, I would like to thank Maria Padilla for coordinating the research materials and working collaboratively with the group facilitators at Centro. Thank you for being a part of this very important work.

In 2015, a new community partner in West Chicago was recruited to conduct groups using the SYP curriculum/program. The West Chicago Police Department offers social services to immigrant Latino families and individuals. One of the services they offer is case management and legal advocacy for immigrant Latina women navigating the criminal justice system. Three groups were conducted between 2015–2016 ($n = 20$). I would like to thank Chief of Police Michael Uplegger for supporting the group facilitators as they conducted the groups and for his pledge to the SYP program. I would also like to thank Rosie Valencia and Eliane Stefango for facilitating the groups and providing feedback with facilitating the program and using the SYP program manual/book. Thank you for your hard work and dedication in recruiting immigrant Latina women in order for them to participate in the SYP program.

Several articles have been published from the doctoral work that made the SYP curriculum/program possible. I would like to acknowledge the external reviewers and editorial assistance conducted by Jodi Swanson for helpful comments on previous versions of manuscripts that spoke to the importance of developing a program for immigrant Latina women who could not reach domestic violence shelters or domestic violence-related community-based agencies. Since the current project began, five articles have been published on the effectiveness of the SYP curriculum/program and one group is scheduled to begin in 2017 at West Chicago Police Department. I was fortunate to have three excellent research assistants who helped me analyze the data, conduct literature reviews, develop tables, and assist in duties related to research tasks. I would like to thank Blaire Hysjulien, Leigh Hartenberg, and Elizabeth Senne for their enthusiasm and quick turnaround on tasks that needed to be completed. Thank you Blaire Hysjulien for creating the logos on the title page.

At Oxford University Press, I would like to acknowledge and thank Senior Editor Dana Bliss for the constructive feedback he shared as I continued to work on the evaluation of the SYP curriculum/program over a two-year period and Andrew Dominello, assistant editor, for his help during the production phase. I would also like to acknowledge and thank Becca Bohnsack at Gathering Waters Design, Inc. in La Crosse, Wisconsin, for providing art design to the Spanish and English illustrations in the SYP program manual/book and Franklin Jauregui for providing Spanish editorial assistance with the illustrations.

The research project was supported by St. Catherine University and the University of St. Thomas School of Social Work in St. Paul, Minnesota. I would like to thank St. Catherine University for providing me with two internal grants that supported the research project. I was fortunate to collect professional feedback about the program from external sources. I am thankful to the faith-based social service program in Minneapolis, which provided professional feedback on the SYP curriculum/program.

The support of mentors and colleagues in the School of Social Work is priceless in the production of writing and conducting research projects. I would like to thank my mentor, Dr. Carol F. Kuechler, who provided long-term insight on my mission-centered scholarly work. Thanks to my colleagues in the School of Social Work, my colleagues in the writing group, and students for their encouragement as I developed and conducted the ongoing research project. Finally, I would like to thank my husband Peter Fuchsel and my family. I am thankful for his thoughtful examination of my work, his endless support as I wrote and worked on edits, and his due diligence in making sure I did my very best. Thank you for all the wonderful conversations in the making of the SYP program manual/book. Thank you to my step-children, Nic, Molly, and Natalie, family members in Arizona, my "Fuchsel" family in Minnesota, and dear friends across the country: they never got tired of supporting my work and hearing about the SYP curriculum/program. I am deeply grateful to my late father, Fred, and my mother, Luz, for believing in my work and devotion to the well-being of Latino families in the United States. Your unconditional love provided me the strength I needed to overcome obstacles along the way. Thank you!

Correspondence and inquiries related to the purchase of the SYP program manual/book should be addressed to Catherine Luz Marrs Fuchsel, PhD, LICSW, LCSW, MSW, at St. Catherine University, 2004 Randolph Avenue, St. Paul, MN, 55105. E-mail: clmarrsfuchsel@stkate.edu

Catherine Luz Marrs Fuchsel, September 2016

PREFACE

I was fortunate to speak Spanish in the United States. Originally from Lima, Peru, I have lived in this country, mainly sunny Arizona, most of my life, and I am bilingual and bicultural. Although I was a young child when I moved to the United States, my parents, Fred and Luz, instilled in me and my four siblings Peruvian values and beliefs. These Peruvian/Latino cultural norms are still a part of me, despite the fact that I align more with American values and beliefs. In my 19-year career as a clinical social worker that began in Detroit, Michigan, I mainly worked with immigrant families from Mexico who lacked legal and immigration status. Being bilingual and bicultural came in handy and was essential in developing relationships and understanding adversity among the families I worked with from a cultural perspective. I was grateful that I spoke Spanish, that I understood the cultural norms, and that I too had migrated, although I was fortunate to have the experience of being a privileged immigrant. I could understand at a deeper level my clients and their experience; I spoke their language, understood their culture, and had an immigrant experience.

After working in New York City at a large children and family service agency with children and adolescents in direct practice, I returned to Arizona to continue my work as a clinical social worker but, more importantly, to return to *mi familia*. I worked at an agency that provided mental health care and services to small children in Phoenix. I helped develop a counseling program for parents and children who participated in Head Start. It was in that experience that I came across the devastating problem of domestic violence, often called intimate partner violence, among the immigrant Mexican women I worked with. The majority of the women I worked with had some kind of relationship problem, often mistaken for depression, anxiety, or aggression, when at the core of the problem was domestic violence in the home. I took every training and course I could through multiple agencies, especially, the Arizona Coalition Against Domestic Violence, to help me understand domestic violence and what women experience. I needed to "walk in their shoes." However, it was the women themselves—my clients who shared their stories with me—who provided the awareness, compassion, and *true* understanding that I needed. That pivotal experience in my career encouraged me to return to academia to obtain my doctorate of philosophy in social work from Arizona State University and to study the phenomena of domestic violence and the meaning of marriage and relationships among immigrant Mexican women. I also promised the women I worked with that I would tell their story and that I would figure out a way to help them get the services they needed. That was 13 years ago.

Since then, I have studied the problem, and I found a way to help them feel better about themselves, understand healthy relationships within a cultural framework, understand domestic violence, and feel empowered to make positive choices and access services. From the findings of my dissertation, I developed a prevention model for immigrant Mexican women, or immigrant Latinas, which became the *Sí, Yo Puedo* (SYP) 11-week curriculum/program for mental health professionals who work with immigrant Latinas in group settings. For the past five years, I have been evaluating the SYP curriculum/program at community-based agencies in two midwestern states. At the core of developing the SYP curriculum/program was finding a way to provide a service, an intervention that immigrant Latina women could access in community-based agencies that were not necessarily shelters or domestic violence crisis centers. Certainly, the SYP curriculum/program can be used in these types of agency settings. I wanted them to receive assistance before they were to the point of needing a shelter or a crisis center. Immigrant Latinas needed help during the relationship. And, even though the majority of them lacked legal and immigration status, they still needed some type of intervention or service that empowered them to access support systems despite these difficult barriers.

This program manual for bilingual Spanish-English mental health professionals is a curriculum that addresses both prevention and intervention for immigrant Latinas, which was started in my direct practice experience with immigrant Mexican women. The SYP curriculum/program has evolved and taken shape through my doctorate training, and I have continued to study and examine it in my current position as a social work educator in the state of Minnesota. The SYP curriculum/program has the potential to change the lives of immigrant Latinas who might be in unhealthy relationships, who want to feel better and have healthy, intimate relationships and families, and who want their children to live without violence in the home. My hope is that mental health professionals such as social workers, counselors, marriage and family therapists, and psychologists from varying disciplines will offer SYP educational and empowerment groups in their practice and in their place of employment, to assist in the overall well-being of immigrant Latina women and their families living in communities across the United States and in other Spanish-speaking countries.

INTRODUCTION TO THE PROGRAM

THE *YES, I CAN* (SÍ, YO PUEDO): *An Empowerment Program for Immigrant Latina Women in Group Settings* (SYP), formerly known as the Domestic Violence Intervention Model curriculum, is an intervention tool to help faciliators create Spanish-speaking psycho-educational groups specifically designed for immigrant Latina women to promote self-esteem, understand healthy romantic relationships, and access resources and support systems in communities. As facilitators cover weekly topics in the psycho-educational groups using instructional teaching methods (e.g., drawing and writing exercises), women can begin the process of self-reflection, assess their self-esteem, and gain an understanding of current romantic relationships and dating experiences within a culturally sensitive and relevant framework. Although immigrant Latina women do not have to be in domestic violence (DV)-related relationships for participation in the program, previous studies suggest that immigrant Latina women in the general population experience high rates of DV (Edelson, Hokoda, & Ramos-Lira, 2007).[1] Thus two classes on healthy relationships and the dynamics of DV are included in the SYP curriculum. Throughout the SYP curriculum, the terms *relationship* and *romantic relationship* are used interchangeably (i.e., a committed, romantic relationship with a partner).

Psycho-educational groups provide immigrant Latina women the opportunity to learn about different topics in the program. Women are invited to share their experiences as they explore various subjects, and they are encouraged to provide support for each other. The facilitator teaches on specific topics and also provides a supportive environment.

IMMIGRANT LATINA WOMEN

The Latino population is the largest and fastest-growing minority group in the United States (U.S. Census Bureau, 2010a).[2] In 2010, an estimated 50.5 million Latinos (including legally immigrated and individuals who lack immigration status) were living in the United States. Nearly 32 million of these identified as Mexican in origin. Among Mexican individuals in the United States, 63% identified as U.S. native-born individuals, whereas 37% identified as foreign-born (U.S. Census Bureau, 2010). Many Latinas residing in the United States identify as Mexican-born and foreign (U.S. Census Bureau, 2010). Although the majority of immigrant Latina women identify as immigrant Mexican women, women born in other Spanish-speaking countries or the United States, and those with other immigrant status, should not be excluded from participating in the groups. Throughout the program manual the terms *immigrant Latina women* and *participants* are used interchangeably.

PREVENTION AND INTERVENTION

Prevention

Several DV-prevention programs with specific curricula (e.g., Expect Respect; Ball, Tharp, Noonan, Valle, Hamburger, & Rosenbluth, 2012)[3] are available in the United States that address prevention strategies for DV and knowledge of healthy dating and relationships for youth. The SYP curriculum and program manual is not specifically targeted for adolescent Latina immigrants or immigrant Latina women who might be in a potentially dangerous *future* romantic relationship but rather for immigrant Latina women who are likely in long-term romantic relationships and who want personal improvement. It is worth noting that the average age of participants in evaluation studies of the SYP program was around 40 years (range = 18–82), and most women reported they were married and lacked legal status.

As group facilitators provide instructional material on the weekly topics, participants are exposed to different types of information. For example, as group facilitators teach on DV, dating, and healthy relationships, participants learn and become aware of what constitutes a healthy relationship and positive dating experiences. Providing education on DV, raising awareness, and helping participants understand support systems and resources are prevention strategies. Nonetheless, the focus of the SYP curriculum is intervention.

Intervention

The main purpose of the SYP program is for participants to experience some type of change in how they feel or think about themselves and their current romantic relationships. As participants learn about different topics, share their experiences with group members, participate in the weekly exercises, and discover how to access resources, change might occur. The goal is that women will change their behavior after completing the SYP program. Thus the SYP curriculum is the intervention component of the SYP program. The SYP curriculum is an intervention measure for immigrant Latinas who want to learn about healthy relationships and DV and use this knowledge to make changes in their current lives and existing relationships. Although a more systematic, multifaceted, complex approach is needed toward ending DV among this unique population, the SYP is a critical first step of exposure and education—both for preventing future DV and for intervening in the lives of those currently affected by DV.

CURRICULUM GOALS

The goals of the curriculum are to (a) increase awareness of DV and what a healthy relationship encompasses, (b) increase self-esteem, (c) increase awareness about current romantic relationships, (d) empower women to reach out for help when applicable, and (e) increase decision-making ability regarding current relationships. Participants may or may not leave a DV relationship as a result of the program, but leaving is not a stated program goal.

CURRICULUM BENEFITS

Educational groups for mental health professionals working with immigrant Latinas

Although other resources exist for professionals serving Latinas experiencing DV (e.g., workshops and trainings offered by the National Latin@ Network; 2015),[4] the SYP curriculum is unique in that it provides a structured step-by-step programmatic guide that is culturally competent for bilingual Spanish-English speaking licensed mental health professionals serving immigrant Latina women who require education and support in developing and maintaining healthy relationships and acquiring a healthy sense of self. In addition, although existing books address counseling techniques and how to work with Latino families in individual therapy generally, there is no structured step-by-step program manual with a specific curriculum that mental health professionals can offer immigrant Latinas who seek peer support, education, and knowledge about healthy relationships and DV in group settings. Practitioners who will find the SYP the most useful are likely those who have experience with group work, who work with immigrant Latinas, and who want to offer psycho-educational groups in addition to individual therapy as a type of intervention throughout the treatment process in direct practice settings. Extending existing programs and books targeted for women who may be experiencing DV, the SYP curriculum approaches intervention from a broader standpoint—it is designed for immigrant Latina women who want to participate in a personal improvement program examining concepts related to self-esteem, healthy relationships, and DV. Participants may not necessarily be in a relationship that is DV-prone. Moreoever, providers do not necessarily need to work in DV-related agencies: Bilingual Spanish-English speaking licensed mental health professionals may work in various social service agencies such as outpatient mental health clinics, community health clinics, faith-based organizations, school programs, or the legal system.

Cultural considerations

Despite the fact that one culturally specific workbook was identified for immigrant Latinas (*Latina Power Workbook*; Nogales, 2010)[5] who experienced incidences of DV, more common are program manuals designed for the general population of women who identify as being in a DV-related relationship in the past or present and who want to learn about healthy relationships and rebuild their lives. Structured step-by step existing program manuals designed for women who identify as being in a DV-related relationship are minimally targeted for the immigrant Latino population and do not take into account cultural considerations such as values, beliefs, and cultural norms predominantly embraced by the Latino community. A contribution of the SYP curriculum is its attention to topics and methods culturally relevant to immigrant Latinas. Cultural topics specifically integrated into the curriculum were derived from previous research examining women's self-esteem, dating patterns, cultural influences on understanding relationships, and how women perceive and understand DV in intimate-partner relationships among immigrant Latinas (Brabeck & Guzmán, 2009; Marrs Fuchsel,

Murphy, & Dufresne, 2012; Vidales, 2010).[6] For example, how *machismo* (i.e., a set of behaviors among Latino males who have characteristics of being dominant, superior, and strong in relationships; Vidales, 2010) and *familism* (i.e., highly integrated families with supportive extended family members; Vidales, 2010) influence DV-prone relationship dynamics is documented in the literature among immigrant Latinas (Brabeck & Guzmán, 2009; Vidales, 2010). Further, the cultural concept of *collectivism* (i.e., values and beliefs encompassing interdependence, belonging, and group cohesion among families, coworkers, and peers; Vidales, 2010) was applied in the development of the group-based intervention, so immigrant Latina women could evaluate themselves based on social norms, family expectations, relationships, and interactions with members of their own group.

Targeting immigrant Latinas in diverse social service agencies

The groups in this program are designed for social service agencies, faith-based programs, legal services in police departments, and community health clinics that provide services to immigrant Latina women in urban and rural cities in the United States. The group meetings are typically conducted in a community-based agency that targets immigrant Latina women who are not in a crisis situation and who are not in a community-based DV shelter or program, though the groups can also be implemented in DV shelters or DV-related programs. Previous studies indicate that immigrant Latina women face challenges in obtaining DV shelters or DV-related services due to immigration status and inability to reach out to formal types of support (Edelson, Hokoda, & Ramos-Lira, 2007).

Often, immigrant Latina women experiencing DV incidences cannot access community-based DV programs and shelters due to language barriers, legal obstacles (e.g., fear of deportation), family obligations, immigration status, or lack of resources (Brabeck, & Guzmán, 2009; Hancock, 2007a; Klevens et al., 2007; Vidales, 2010).[7] In addition, by providing psycho-educational groups in diverse social service agency settings, immigrant Latina women who lack immigration status will most likely be targeted. The ability to provide an intervention program with a specific, culturally competent curriculum outside of community-based DV programs and shelters offers immigrant Latina women access to educational groups in community settings that will help them gain knowledge on DV, understand the importance of safety planning and accessing resources, and become empowered to create changes in their lives.

Finally, another important benefit is implementing the SYP program in Spanish. Immigrant Latina women can share their experiences with participants in their native language. Participants who learn more about healthy relationships and DV in a group format (i.e., instruction from the group facilitator and support from group members) are expected to examine current partners and consider some kind of personal change.

CHALLENGES TO PROGRAM PARTICIPATION

Despite the benefits of the SYP curriculum and program, one central challenge is recruitment of immigrant Latinas for participation. Immigrant Latinas living in both rural and urban settings might find it difficult to participate because of lack of direct services in their native language. Another challenge is implementing this kind of program in a non-DV community-based agency or shelter setting. Participants may have diverse experiences with DV and may feel reluctant to disclose in a community setting, specifically immigrant Latinas who might lack immigration status because of fear of involvement with the police department; however, immigrant Latinas who are exposed to the program are encouraged to share experiences somewhat candidly, because the group is completely confidential and anonymous.

CURRICULUM OUTCOMES

After completion of the 11-week psycho-educational group using the SYP curriculum, immigrant Latina women will likely have gained (a) awareness of DV and what constitutes a healthy relationship, (b) behavioral change regarding being able to detect early signs of DV incidences in dating or in current romantic relationships, (c) attitudinal change regarding self-awareness on the type of relationship they wish to engage in, and (d) increased self-esteem.

SYP CURRICULUM AND WEEKLY TOPICS

The SYP curriculum is a culturally competent psycho-educational Spanish-speaking program designed for immigrant Latina women in a two-hour weekly group format. The program is 11 weeks long, with 10 weeks of material and an 11th graduation session. Each session includes an introduction to the weekly topics, drawing and writing reflection exercises, sharing of drawing and writing pieces, and instruction on the topics. The drawing and writing exercises are designed to help women experience self-reflection and self-awareness about identity, self-esteem, and how they view current romantic relationships.

Topics addressing issues related to immigrant Latina women's sense of self, characteristics of healthy relationships and dating, understanding the dynamics of DV, and accessing resources are grouped into three major parts of the curriculum. Part I covers *Awareness of Self* (i.e., Who Am I?, Coping Strategies, Self-esteem, Influences of Past Trauma). Part II covers *Knowledge of Relationships within Culture* (i.e., Dating; Cultural Concepts: *Familism, Machismo,* and *Marianismo;* Healthy Relationships; and Domestic Violence. Part III comprises *Impact of Factors on Relationships* (i.e., Factors Influencing Relationships, Talking to Children, and Resources/Graduation). Table I.1 depicts the three major parts of the curriculum, topics, instructional methods, and types of drawing and writing exercises and activities.

The 11 sessions are intended to be completed in the specified order. Topics should not be switched around, because each session builds on the previous one. In addition, the ordering of the sessions complements the stages of group work (Toseland & Rivas, 2017)[8]: In the initial stages of group work, members begin the process of getting to know each other and begin to develop trust. In the middle stages of group work, group members are more comfortable with each other, sharing stories and providing emotional support to each other. Finally, in the end stage of group work, group members learn about different topics and experience the processes of empowerment and change together.

Table I.1 SYP CURRICULUM AND WEEKLY TOPICS

		Large-Group Discussion	Instruction/Psycho-Education: Instruction on Topics	Self-Reflection Drawing or Writing Activity
Part I: Awareness of Self	Week 1: Introductions Who Am I?	Identity and awareness of self	Values and beliefs	Who am I? folder activity
	Week 2: Coping Strategies	Coping strategies	Definition of coping and positive and negative coping strategies; relaxation and deep breathing exercises	Identify four problems and related coping strategies
	Week 3: Self-esteem	Identify self-esteem	Definition of self-esteem and assessment of current self-esteem	What do you think and how do you feel about yourself?
	Week 4: Influences of Past Traumas	Influences of past traumas on women's sense of self	Dynamics and definition of sexual abuse, child abuse, or other types of traumas as identified by the participants	Timeline activity
Part II: Knowledge of Relationship within Culture	Week 5: Dating	Dynamics of dating experiences within the Latino culture	Characteristics of healthy dating	What does dating look like? Draw or write about your first dating experience.
	Week 6: Cultural Concepts: *Familism, Machismo, and Marianismo*	Cultural concepts and how that impacts participant's knowledge of dating and healthy relationships	Knowledge of *familism, machismo,* and *marianismo*	Draw a picture or write about cultural concepts influencing relationships. Alternate: Genogram/ identify family patterns.
	Week 7: Healthy Relationships	Healthy relationships	Characteristics of healthy relationships; Use equality wheel handout; healthy relationships characteristics handout.	Draw a picture of how you view your current relationship.
	Week 8: Domestic Violence	Domestic violence	Dynamics, definition, types of abuse found in domestic violence, legal issues, and overall prevalence rates	None
Part III: Impact of Factors on Relationships	Week 9: Factors Influencing Relationships	Factors that influence women's understanding of relationships	Specific factors such as the media, parents, and religious institutions	Factors; are they positive or negative influences?
	Week 9: Alternate Topic: Sexual Abuse	Impact of childhood sexual abuse on adult relationships	Definition of childhood sexual abuse, how to protect children (e.g, signs to look for), and how to access resources in the community	None
	Week 10: Talking to Children	Women's ability to talk to their children (girls and boys) about healthy dating	Sensitive topics such as healthy communication and relationships with children and teenagers	Draw a picture of a crystal ball and write a letter to your child. What will you say?
	Week 11: Resources and Graduation	Empowerment and changes	Safety measures and mental health/domestic violence resource handout	Suitcase activity: What will you take with you? Meal, graduation, presentation of certificate, group members exchange phone numbers.

Table created by author.

NOTES

1. Edelson, M. G., Hokoda, A., & Ramos-Lira, L. (2007). Differences in effects of domestic violence between Latina and non-Latina women. *Journal of Family Violence, 22*, 1–10. doi:10.1007/s10896-006-9051-1

2. U.S. Census Bureau. (2010a). *Current population survey: Annual social and economic supplement.* Retrieved February 20, 2012, from http://www.census.gov/population/www/socdemo/hispanic/reports.html

3. Ball, B., Tharp, A. T., Noonan, R. K., Valle, L. A., Hamburger, M. E., & Rosenbluth, B. (2012). Expect Respect support group: Preliminary evaluation of a dating violence prevention program for at-risk youth. *Violence Against Women, 18*, 746–762. doi:10.1177/1077801212455188

4. *National Latin@ Network.* (n.d.). Retrieved October 28, 2015, from National Latin@ Network: http://www.nationallatinonetwork.org/

5. Nogales, D. A. (2010). *Latina power: Using your 7 strengths to say no to abusive relationships– a Latina power workbook.* Author.

6. Brabeck, K. M., & Guzmán, M. R. (2009). Exploring Mexican-origin intimate partner abuse survivors' help-seeking within their sociocultural contexts. *Violence and Victims, 24*, 817–832. doi:10.1891/0886-6708.24.6.817; Marrs Fuchsel, C., Murphy, S., & Dufresne, R. (2012). Domestic violence, culture, and relationship dynamics among immigrant Mexican women. *Affilia: Journal of Women and Social Work, 27*, 263–274. doi:10.1177/0886109912452403; Vidales, G. T. (2010). Arrested justice: The multifaceted plight of immigrant Latinas who faced domestic violence. *Journal of Family Violence, 25*, 533–544. doi:10.1007/s10896-010-93095

7. Hancock, T. (2007a). Addressing wife abuse in Mexican immigrant couples: Challenges for family social workers. *Journal of Family Social Work, 10*, 31–50. doi:10.1300/J039v10n03_03; Klevens, J., Shelley, G., Clavel-Arcas, C., Barney, D. D., Tobar, C., Duran, E. S., Barajas-Mazaheri, R., & Esparza, J. (2007). Latinos' perspectives and experiences with intimate partner violence. *Violence Against Women, 13*, 141–158. doi:10.1177/1077801206296980

8. Toseland, R. W., & Rivas, R. F. (2017). *An introduction to group work practice: Connecting core competencies series* (8th ed.). Boston, MA: Pearson Education.

1

DEVELOPMENT OF THE SYP CURRICULUM

BACKGROUND INFORMATION

A culturally competent *Sí, Yo Puedo* (SYP) curriculum, formerly known as the Domestic Violence Intervention Model curriculum, was developed from a larger study that examined several hypotheses on how to work with immigrant Mexican women who may be experiencing domestic violence (DV) and how immigrant Mexican women living with DV perceive and process DV and the marriage institution (Marrs Fuchsel et al., 2012).[1] In-depth structured interviews and a thematic analysis of the findings were conducted among a group of immigrant Mexican women. An important component of these hypotheses was the examination of DV and relationship dynamics within a culturally specific framework. For example, cultural concepts relevant to immigrant Mexican women, such as *familism* and *machismo*, have influenced dating patterns and knowledge about relationships.

Vidales (2010)[2] examined the multiple challenges faced by immigrant Latinas experiencing DV and addressed how cultural beliefs such as *machismo* and traditional gender roles affected their perceptions of DV and help-seeking behaviors. Findings indicated women were more accepting of traditional gender roles and were influenced by negative characteristics of *machismo*. Topics on *machismo* were included in the curriculum because immigrant Mexican women's perception of *machismo*, in particular, likely influences their experiences with dating, relationships, and self-esteem.

The cultural influence of *familism* may also be a contributing factor in Latinas' decision to report or ability to report incidences of DV (Edelson, Hokoda, & Ramos-Lira, 2007; Ulibarri, Ulloa, & Camacho, 2009; Vidales, 2010).[3] On the one hand, *familism* may serve as a protective factor for the victim as she reaches out for emotional support. On the other hand, the victim may be embarrassed or ashamed to reach out for help because immigrant Mexican women may be reluctant to disrupt the family unity (Marrs Fuchsel, 2013).[4] It was important to include the cultural concept of *familism* in the curriculum because *familism* is embedded in the lives of immigrant Latina women and may impact their ability to reach out for help and access resources. Another term explored was the concept of *marianismo* (i.e., an idea or set of beliefs rooted in Catholicism that refers to the mother [the Virgin Mary] of Jesus and that signifies women's experiences with the meaning and concept of submissiveness in relationships; Marrs Fuchsel et al., 2012).[5] In Marrs Fuchsel et al.'s (2012) study, only one participant was familiar with the term *marianismo*. It would be reasonable to assume that an immigrant Mexican women who wants to keep her family intact and who might be influenced by *marianismo* would choose to separate from a DV-prone partner; however, for this participant, understanding of the concept may be skewed—she might believe that being submissive is part of her role as wife and mother, and it might influence her decision to keep her family together, despite incidences of DV. The information was limited because eight of the nine participants had never heard the term before; therefore, it was difficult to make comparisons with regard to whether the term was accurately represented. Further investigation is needed on whether sexually aggressive behaviors are part of the concept of *machismo* and if there is a direct relationship between the cultural scripts (*machismo* and *marianismo*) and DV incidences.

In addition, membership in religious institutions (e.g., the Catholic Church) may influence immigrant Latina women's decisions to reach out for help when experiencing DV in current relationships because oftentimes immigrant Latinas discuss marriage and relationship issues with parish priests (Marrs Fuchsel, 2012).[6] Although not all immigrant Latina women identify as Catholic, immigrant Latina women often turn to the Catholic Church for support and prefer to discuss a DV situation with a priest (Marrs Fuchsel, 2012). These components (i.e., *familism*, *machismo*, *marianismo*, and the influence of religious institutions) of the culturally specific hypotheses were included in the development of the curriculum and are specifically addressed in Part II of the SYP curriculum (Marrs Fuchsel et al., 2012).

Although the original study was a single, qualitative study with a small sample (n = 9; Marrs Fuchsel et al., 2012),[7] subsequent studies examining the effectiveness of the SYP curriculum have utilized multiple research designs such as rigorous qualitative methods (i.e., action research) and a mixed-methods design (i.e., qualitative and quantitative research), conducted across a five-year period (2011–2016). So far, 88 immigrant Latina women have completed the SYP program in eleven groups with three community partners in two Midwestern states (i.e., Minnesota and Illinois).

LESSONS LEARNED FROM A PILOT TEST AND AN ONGOING LONGITUDINAL EVALUATION

In 2011–2012, a qualitative exploratory study was conducted to examine the experiences of immigrant Latina women using the SYP curriculum in a Midwestern state (Marrs Fuchsel & Hysjulien, 2013).[8] Using a psycho-educational group format, 20 immigrant Latina women participated in two 11-week groups over a nine-month period at a community-based health clinic. Findings indicated immigrant Latina women examined current relationships, dating, and DV dynamics in group settings and reported changes in self-esteem within their own culture.

Qualitative investigations of immigrant Latina participants' experiences with the SYP curriculum indicated that it was the specific content material as opposed to group dynamics (e.g., dynamics of DV, self-esteem, coping strategies, past traumas, cultural concepts, dating; Marrs Fuchsel & Hysjulien, 2013) that immigrant Latinas found most helpful in each of the sessions. For example, one participant stated: "What was most helpful in this class was learning how the *family* is the foundation of happiness in human beings, but also, a bad family can destroy the others in the family and the [marriage] relationship." Another participant described a negative impact of *machismo*: "Just because he [husband] is 'macho' does not mean he can treat me that way [using verbal abuse]." In addition, participants provided weekly feedback on how to improve the SYP program by filling out a written questionnaire. In their feedback, participants described the importance of including prevalence rates of DV among immigrant Latinas and how to access legal information. Implications for mental health professionals (e.g., social workers) included learning how they can use culturally competent curriculums and programs in group formats.

RIGOROUS QUALITATIVE RESEARCH AND LONGITUDINAL ANALYSIS OF THE SYP PROGRAM

Follow-up groups

Two follow-up groups with participants from the original pilot study (one at 6 months and one at 12 months) were conducted in 2012 (*n* = 14; Marrs Fuchsel; 2014a)[9] and given a written questionnaire with five open-ended questions to examine how participants felt about themselves and current romantic relationships after completing the SYP program. Participants described experiencing the process of empowerment and wanting to make changes in their lives, such as returning to school, seeking employment, and asking their partners to change their behavior. Others described losing weight, enrolling in educational classes, and thinking about short- and long-term goals for themselves. One participant stated:

> My self-esteem improved a lot because I was in a situation where I didn't care if my husband offended me. Thanks to the group, I decided to make a list of my short- and long-term goals and achieve them one by one. I love myself more, I'm taking care of myself, and I am succeeding thanks to God and to the program.

Participants credited participation in the SYP program with improvement in self-esteem in both of the groups, regardless of when participants completed the program. The participants reported feeling better and taking the necessary steps to make positive changes in their lives.

Action research

In 2011–2013, four groups (i.e., Groups 1–4) were conducted at a Minnesota community health clinic (*n* = 36) using action research (Marrs Fuchsel, 2014b),[10] a type of qualitative research that incorporates working with community-based agencies throughout the research process. Community-based agencies identify a need and an area of study that is important to the agency in the hopes of promoting social justice and some type of change. Key stakeholders in community-based agencies work together with the researcher and research team to identify the research question, research method, type of data analysis, and implications of the study for the community-based agency (Marrs Fuchsel, 2014a).

Findings indicated the importance of providing a psycho-educational program such as the SYP program for patients at the community health clinic. The majority of the patients served at the community health clinic were immigrant Latinos of Mexican descent. Medical providers indicated that patients disclosed symptoms of depression and anxiety, relationship problems, and parenting issues, as well as incidences of DV, past child abuse, and traumatic events during medical appointments. The community-based agency did not offer mental health services; however, the clinic administrator wanted to offer psycho-educational groups for patients that were culturally sensitive and that examined concepts related to self-esteem, healthy relationships, dating, and knowledge of DV.

Patients who participated in the SYP program reported increases in their understanding of DV and healthy relationships. For example, one participant reported: "Now I understand even more that no human being, no matter how stressed, deserves to be treated with violence of any type. I should respect myself and make others respect and value me as a woman." Another participant described the importance of parental involvement with children as they ask questions related to healthy relationships and DV. The participant stated: "Violence shouldn't be tolerated. Now we have more knowledge of the different ways in which we can classify something as 'domestic violence,' whether it is physical, verbal, emotional, etc., we have good knowledge to teach our children."

Participants reported the ability to detect early signs of DV in dating relationships and understand the types of relationships they wanted. One participant stated: "Nobody has the right to mistreat you, everything begins at home and during dating. I now have the resources and tools if I need them and I know where to go." Another conveyed: "Domestic violence occurs in many forms and it can happen to anyone. Dating is hard, but it can help us have a good relationship in the long run." Although the majority of the participants did not report on how they feel and think about options that might help in decision-making about current or past relationships, a few reported that options were available in making decisions about current relationships.

Mixed-methods design 1

In 2013–2014, two more groups (i.e., Groups 5 and 6; $n = 14$) were conducted at another community-based agency in an urban city in Minnesota (Marrs Fuchsel, Linares, Abugattas, Padilla, & Hartenberg, 2015).[11] The community-based agency in Minnesota provides educational and health programs for Latino families and promotes Latino cultural norms and values. The *summative evaluative framework* (i.e., determining the success of a program for future use; Monette, Sullivan, & DeJong, 2014)[12] was examined because researchers were interested in testing the effectiveness of the SYP curriculum and program. In this study, a pre-and posttest survey was administered at the beginning and end of the SYP program to assess for differences in self-esteem and knowledge and attitudes toward DV before versus after program participation. Once again, participants were invited to provide open-ended feedback on their overall experience with the SYP program. Results from a paired t-test ($t[13] = 4.49$, $p < .001$; 95% confidence intervals = 2.56, 7.30) indicated that self-esteem scores at posttest ($M = 24.29$, $SD = 3.38$) were significantly greater than self-esteem scores at the pretest ($M = 19.36$, $SD = 4.22$; Marrs Fuchsel et al., 2015).[13]

Qualitative analysis indicated that almost half of the participants stated that in learning about the types of abuse (e.g., verbal, physical, financial), the danger signs and saying no to DV was important. Examples are "Well, I think we should not let anyone abuse us; we have to value ourselves as women"; "Now I am more aware of the danger signs and I have more confidence in myself to stop situations in my relationship when they are not going well." By understanding the different types of abuse and characteristics of healthy relationships, the participants became more aware of their own relationships. Participants reported feeling more confident in saying *no* to their partners during disputes and wanting to have better communication with partners: "I think it is important not to fight and argue with derogatory words. It is better to dialogue with respect and confidence." The majority of the participants identified what they wanted (i.e., additional support and a relationship without DV), and they began to think about their future.

Mixed-methods design 2

Groups 7 and 8 were completed (*n* = 14) in 2015 with another community partner in the state of Illinois, a police department situated in a suburb of the city of Chicago. The bilingual Spanish-English licensed mental health professional works with immigrant Latinas who need resources and a support system as they navigate the criminal justice system. In this study, a mixed-methods design was administered with a new pre- and posttest survey that included culturally sensitive questions related to knowledge and attitudes toward DV in working with Latina immigrants. Twelve participants were included in this quantitative assessment. Using a standard paired *t*-test, the first test conducted examined whether the SYP increased self-esteem in immigrant Latina women. Participants' self-esteem scores were significantly higher at postassessment (*M* = 22.42, *SD* = 5.20) than at preassessment (*M* = 18.25, *SD* = 4.83), *t*(11) = −4.17, *p* = .03 (Marrs Fuchsel, Valencia, Stefango, Uplegger, & Sennes, 2016).[14]

Findings from the culturally sensitive survey (e.g., two items from the 17-item survey) indicated a difference in accessing informal and formal types of support systems. In item 14, "What would you tell a friend whose spouse or partner was beating him or her? Check off all that apply, with a maximum of three responses below," descriptive analysis indicated a positive change in frequency from preassessment to postassessment. In the preassessment, 6 (43%) participants indicated, "Turn him in to authorities," whereas in the postassessment, 11 (79%) participants reported they would tell a friend to contact the police. In addition, despite the fact that item 15 (i.e., "Do you know of a place [or places] where a person can go to get help if he or she is being beaten by his or her spouse or partner?") did not show any statistically significant change in the percentage responding "yes" from preassessment to postassessment, descriptive analysis indicated an increase in frequency on formal types of support. In the pretest survey, 11 (79%) participants indicated reaching out to police officers for help, whereas in the postassessment, 13 (93%) participants reported contacting the police. In the pretest survey, 4 participants indicated reaching out to DV shelters, whereas in the posttest, 10 (71%) participants reported contacting DV shelters (Marrs Fuchsel, et al., 2016).[15]

Group facilitator's experience using the SYP curriculum

Six group facilitators used the SYP program in the five-year research project. All were Spanish-English speaking graduate-level licensed mental health professionals and identified as understanding the Latino culture. For example, two of the group facilitators (i.e., a licensed independent clinical social worker and a licensed marriage and family therapist) were from Peru, one group facilitator (i.e., a licensed marriage and family therapist) was from Columbia, another group facilitator (i.e., a social worker) was from Panama, and another group facilitator (i.e., a licensed clinical psychologist) was from Brazil. The majority of the group facilitators lived in the United States for more than 20 years. One group facilitator was an intern, and she conducted two sessions (i.e., at the time, she was working toward her master's in counseling degree) and identified as bilingual and bicultural as she was born in Chicago to immigrant parents (from Michoacán, Mexico). We conducted five in-depth semistructured interviews, participant observation, and reflexivity (i.e., the process of reflecting on oneself as the researcher, the research relationship, and the process as the researcher conducts interviews; Monette, Sullivan, & DeJong, 2014)[16] as methods of collecting data on group facilitator's experience using the SYP curriculum and program. The author of the SYP program conducted the first four groups.

Between 2015–2016, group 9 and 10 ($n = 18$) was completed at the community-based agency in Minnesota, and group 11 was completed at the police department in Illinois ($n = 7$). Over a five-year period, eleven groups were completed ($n = 88$), with over 80 immigrant Latina women participating in the SYP program. Rigorous qualitative research designs such as action research and mixed-method designs were used in the evaluation of the SYP curriculum and program manual. In addition, the experiences of the group facilitator's use of the SYP curriculum and program provided insight and information on the structure of the curriculum, the weekly topics, and the facilitation of the groups. Almost 100 immigrant Latina women participated in the SYP program, and positive results, such as change in knowledge and attitudes toward DV and improvement in self-esteem and personal growth, were reported.

NOTES

1. Marrs Fuchsel, C., Murphy, S., & Dufresne, R. (2012). Domestic violence, culture, and relationship dynamics among immigrant Mexican women. *Affilia: Journal of Women and Social Work, 27*, 263–274. doi:10.1177/0886109912452403

2. Vidales, G. T. (2010). Arrested justice: The multifaceted plight of immigrant Latinas who faced domestic violence. *Journal of Family Violence, 25*, 533–544. doi:10.1007/s10896-010-93095

3. Edelson, M. G., Hokoda, A., & Ramos-Lira, L. (2007). Differences in effects of domestic violence between Latina and non-Latina women. *Journal of Family Violence, 22*, 1–10. doi:10.1007/s10896-006-9051-1; Ulibarri, M. D., Ulloa, E. C., & Camacho, L. (2009). Prevalence of sexually abusive experiences in childhood and adolescence among a community sample of Latinas: A descriptive study. *Journal of Child Sexual Abuse, 18*, 405–421. doi:10.1080/10538710903051088; Vidales, G. T. (2010). Arrested justice: The multifaceted plight of immigrant Latinas who faced domestic violence. *Journal of Family Violence, 25*, 533–544. doi:10.1007/s10896-010-93095

4. Marrs Fuchsel, C. (2013). *Familism*, sexual abuse, and domestic violence among immigrant Mexican women. *Affilia: Journal of Women and Social Work, 28*, 378–389. doi:10.1177/0886109913503265

5. Marrs Fuchsel, C., Murphy, S., & Dufresne, R. (2012). Domestic violence, culture, and relationship dynamics among immigrant Mexican women. *Affilia: Journal of Women and Social Work, 27*, 263–274. doi:10.1177/0886109912452403

6. Marrs Fuchsel, C. (2012). The Catholic Church as a support for immigrant Mexican women living with domestic violence. *Social Work & Christianity, 39*(1), 66–87.

7. Marrs Fuchsel, C., Murphy, S., & Dufresne, R. (2012). Domestic violence, culture, and relationship dynamics among immigrant Mexican women. *Affilia: Journal of Women and Social Work, 27*, 263–274. doi:10.1177/0886109912452403

8. Marrs Fuchsel, C., & Hysjulien, B. (2013). Exploring a domestic violence intervention curriculum for immigrant Mexican women in a group setting: A pilot study. *Social Work with Groups, 36*, 304–320. doi 10.1080/01609513.2013.767130

9. Marrs Fuchsel, C. (2014a). Exploratory evaluation of *Sí, Yo Puedo*: A culturally competent empowerment program for immigrant Latina women in group settings. *Social Work with Groups, 37*, 279–296. doi:10.1080/01609513.2014.895921

10. Marrs Fuchsel, C. (2014b). "Yes, I have changed because I am more sure of myself, I feel stronger with more confidence and strength": Examining the experiences of immigrant Latina women participating in the *Sí, Yo Puedo* curriculum. *Journal of Ethnographic and Qualitative Research, 8*, 161–182.

11. Marrs Fuchsel, C., Linares, R., Abugattas, A., Padilla, M., & Hartenberg, L. (2015). *Sí, Yo Puedo* curricula: Latinas examining domestic violence and self. *Affilia: Journal of Women and Social Work, 31*, 219–231. doi:10.1177/0886109915608220

12. Monette, D. R., Sullivan, T. J. & DeJong, C. R. (2014). *Applied social research: Tool for the human services* (9th ed.). Belmont, CA: Brooks/Cole.

13. Marrs Fuchsel, C., Linares, R., Abugattas, A., Padilla, M., & Hartenberg, L. (2015). *Sí, Yo Puedo* curricula: Latinas examining domestic violence and self. *Affilia: Journal of Women and Social Work, 31*, 219–231. doi:10.1177/0886109915608220

14. Marrs Fuchsel, C., Valencia, R., Stefango, E., Uplegger, M., & Sennes, E. (2016). *Sí, Yo Puedo* curricula and police departments: Educating immigrant Latinas. *Affilia, Journal of Women and Social Work*. Epub May 16, doi:10.1080/01609513.2017.1318329

15. Ibid.

16. Monette, D. R., Sullivan, T. J. & DeJong, C. R. (2014). *Applied social research: Tool for the human services* (9th ed.). Belmont, CA: Brooks/Cole.

UNDERSTANDING DOMESTIC VIOLENCE AMONG IMMIGRANT LATINA WOMEN

2

AVAILABLE LITERATURE ON IMMIGRANT LATINA WOMEN AND domestic violence (DV) focuses on prevalence and rates, help-seeking behaviors, the impact of immigration status on DV experiences, transnational elements and DV, types of support systems available to immigrant Latina women, barriers immigrant Latina women encounter as they access services (e.g., inability to speak the language or fear of deportation), and how cultural concepts such as *familism, machismo,* and *marianismo* likely contribute to immigrant Latina women's experiences with DV (Edelson, Hokoda, & Ramos-Lira, 2007; Hancock, 2007a, 2007b; Hancock & Ames, 2008; Kasturirangan, Krishnan, & Riger, 2004; Perilla, 1999; Vidales, 2010).[1]

PREVALENCE AND BARRIERS TO REPORTING

Approximately 1 in 4 (24.3%) U.S. women are severely assaulted (e.g., physical violence) and nearly half of all women (48%) experience psychological abuse by male partners each year (Black et al., 2011).[2] Additionally, most U.S. women (69%) experience DV before the age of 25 (i.e., more DV incidents than any other age group; Black et al., 2011).[3] DV is a prevalent problem for women living in the United States, yet little is known about how cultural dynamics influence DV experiences for immigrant Latina women. Within the past 10 years, researchers have begun to study DV experiences among the Latino population within a sociocultural context (i.e., race/ethnicity, socioeconomic status, cultural concepts, religion; Brabeck & Guzmán, 2009; Kasturirangan, et al., 2004; Klevens et al., 2007; Vidales, 2010).[4] By incorporating these factors in the study of DV, researchers and practitioners can gain different perspectives on the prevention and intervention of DV, resulting in a fuller understanding of the problem.

Statistical data on rates of DV among immigrant Latina women is limited because of underreporting to law enforcement agencies and the need for more refined categories in obtaining statistical data on the prevalence of DV among types of groups that fall under the umbrella of *Latino/Hispanic* (Edelson, Hokoda, & Ramos-Lira, 2007; Frias & Angel, 2005; Hancock, 2007a).[5] Results from the National Violence Against Women Survey indicated that Latinos experience 23% of DV incidences in their lifetime (Klevens, 2007),[6] and Latina women living in rural parts of the United States, 20% experience incidences of DV (Klevens, 2007).

Poverty, low education, poor English proficiency, a failure to understand mainstream U.S. cultural norms, and lacking immigration status are barriers to immigrant Latina women's help-seeking behaviors (Brabeck & Guzmán, 2009; Frias & Angel, 2005; Vidales, 2010).[7] In addition, women's responses to abuse and how they manage incidences of DV vary by ethnicity for Latina women versus non-Latina women (Brabeck & Guzmán, 2008, 2009; Edelsen et al., 2007; Klevens,

2007).[8] For example, immigrant Latina women who lack legal status might be less likely to report incidences of abuse because of fear of deportation (Brabeck & Guzmán, 2009).[9] With regard to immigrant Latina women's experiences with DV, family social workers are encouraged to discuss the importance of responding to incidences of DV within a cultural perspective and how that plays a role in the outcome of how couples manage problems related to DV (Hancock, 2007a; Vidales, 2010).[10]

HELP-SEEKING BEHAVIORS AMONG IMMIGRANT LATINA WOMEN

Gender roles and cultural traditions that do not encourage women's empowerment or independence, lack of English proficiency, lack of culturally sensitive services for immigrant Latinas, and lack of immigration status are all barriers to the help-seeking behaviors for this population of women who are experiencing incidences of DV (Reina, Lohman, & Maldonado, 2014; Sabina, Cuevas, & Schally, 2012).[11] Sabina et al. (2012), who examined help-seeking behaviors among victimized Latinas in a national sample (n = 714) of Latino women, found that 69% of the participants engaged in help-seeking behavior with informal resources (i.e., reaching out to family, friends, and clergy), but only 33% utilized formal resources (i.e., contacting the police department or programs in community-based agencies; Sabina et al., 2012).

Because members of the immigrant Latina population are less likely to seek help in formal organizations and entities, the *Sí, Yo Puedo* (SYP) curriculum and program is designed to serve this group in informal settings such as health-care community clinics, faith-based organizations, or family service centers. Recruitment methods such as word-of-mouth and talking to family, friends, or clergy members (i.e., informal resources) about the SYP program have proven to be powerful techniques and positive recruitment methods in evaluation research. Immigrant Latina women who learned about the SYP program in these types of settings tended to encourage their friends to participate, whereas compared to a more formal programs and settings (e.g., outpatient mental health clinics, DV shelters, police departments), immigrant Latinas might hesitate to access formal resources (Sabina et al., 2012).[12] Immigrant Latina women can participate in the SYP program even when they are not accessing formal resources and, importantly, regardless of their immigration status.

Because of the barriers in accessing formal resources, the need for the SYP curriculum and program is justifiable. The SYP program can be used to educate and empower immigrant Latinas to access formal resources. For example, as participants learn about healthy relationships and DV, the group facilitator teaches them how to access legal resources and how to contact police officers in severe DV incidences regardless of immigration status. Participants learn about orders of protection, U visas, and applying for a change in immigration status if they were victims of DV in past or current relationships.

LEGAL SERVICES AND THE IMPACT OF IMMIGRATION STATUS

Familiarity with the varied and diverse contextual circumstances affecting immigrant Latina women is critical for group facilitators. These include knowledge regarding DV among immigrant Latina women, prevalence and barriers to reporting, help-seeking behaviors, legal services and the impact of immigration status, and transnational family concerns. By having this type of awareness, group facilitators can tailor the weekly topics to these kinds of experiences and offer support to those who might be experiencing these kinds of issues specifically.

Legal services

A handful of investigations have addressed immigrant Latina women's experience with the Violence Against Women Act (VAWA), legislation that aids women who lack immigration status with incidences of DV. Immigrant Latina women who lack immigration status can file for a U visa (i.e., an application for legal status to reside and work in the United States) if she can prove that she is in a good-faith marriage to a legal resident and is experiencing incidences of DV (Goldman, 1999; Parmley, 2004; U.S. Department of Justice, 2015).[13] Despite this, the number of U visa applications filed remains low, perhaps because women in committed relationships are not legally married to U.S. citizens, lack knowledge about VAWA resources, lack transportation, or are afraid of deportation (Goldman, 1999; Parmley, 2004).[14] In addition to VAWA providing legal resources to immigrant Latina women, other resources such as access to public benefits are available under the Immigration and Nationality Act (Broder, 2005).[15]

Immigration services and access to public benefits

Under the Immigration and Nationality Act, an immigrant who is a victim of DV may be able to apply for Suspension of Deportation or Cancellation of Removal (U.S. Department of Justice, 2015).[16] Furthermore, under the guidelines of VAWA, immigrant Latina women and children may be considered for *qualified immigrant* status under the Welfare Act and might be eligible to apply for public benefits (Broder, 2005; Legal Momentum Advancing Women's Rights, 2005),[17] such as Social Security income, healthcare, and other types of aid, such as Temporary Assistance to Needy Families or the Supplemental Nutrition Assistance Program (Broder, 2005; Legal Momentum Advancing Women's Rights, 2005). As SYP program group facilitators discuss legal resources and information regarding immigration status and experiences of DV in the weekly sessions (i.e., Healthy Relationships and Domestic Violence sessions), immigrant Latina women learn more about their rights and are more empowered to access formal types of resources.

Transnational elements for immigrant Latinas experiencing DV

Another important consideration for immigrant Latina women is the transnational experiences of women who manage their families in two separate countries (e.g., the United States and Mexico). The term *transnational migrant* is used to identify a group of individuals who "live their lives across [national] borders" (Furman & Negi, 2007, p. 107).[18] Immigrant Latina women from Latin America, Central America, Spanish-speaking islands such as Puerto Rico and the Dominican Republic, and Mexico often migrate to the United States for employment opportunities, to reunite with family members living in the United States, and to escape a DV relationship in their home country (Alcalde, 2010; Dominguez & Lubitow, 2008; Furman & Negi, 2007).[19] Although the transnational experience for immigrant Latinas can oftentimes be a positive experience (e.g., securing employment, keeping family ties intact despite the distance, providing financial assistance to family members in their home country), immigrant Latinas face challenges with living across two borders (Alcalde, 2010; Dominguez & Lubitow, 2008).

For example, in Dominguez and Lubitow's (2008)[20] study using ethnographic longitudinal interviews and participant observation with 11 Latin American women living in severe poverty, an important finding included the benefits of social support and family connections and minimal isolation in the lives of immigrant Latinas. Although there was a strong social support system, such as the ability to communicate with family members in two countries using the telephone, e-mail communication, and occasional visits to the home country, one participant in a DV-prone relationship experienced isolation. The participant's partner was very controlling (e.g., screening phone calls), prevented the participant from making friends, and was verbally abusive. Despite the fact that the partner exhibited controlling behaviors, the participant reached out to family members for support in her home country.

Another challenge immigrant Latinas face living across borders while experiencing DV is deportation threats from their partners, a type of DV, when living in the United States (Alcalde, 2010).[21] Immigrant Latina women often do not understand how these types of deportation threats can be seen as a type of DV. Finally, immigrant Latinas experience transnational parenting (i.e., parenting across borders as children are often left with family members in their home country; Alcalde, 2010). Immigrant Latina women maintain social ties and connections with their children with the hope of bringing their children to the United States in the near future.

Former participants in the SYP program often discussed concerns about transnational matters. As participants discussed types of social support and informal resources such as reaching out to family members, they described their challenges with family members living in other countries. It is important for group facilitators to understand and address transnational elements among immigrant Latina women as they teach in the weekly topics because it might require flexibility with the topic and successful facilitation of group dynamics. Openly addressing these important experiences (i.e., transnationalism) can offer a means for social support to those participants who self-disclose.

DOMESTIC VIOLENCE PROGRAMS AND INTERVENTIONS IN COMMUNITY-BASED AGENCIES

To date, there are limited number of intervention programs for women experiencing DV-related incidences with partners in non-community-based DV shelters or agencies with a focus on helping women manage DV-related incidences (Allen & Wozniak, 2011; McPhail, Busch, Kulkarni, & Rice, 2007; Whitaker et al., 2007.)[22] Although few investigators have examined the benefits of support groups for Latina women in community-based DV shelters or agency settings, culturally competent programs for immigrant Latina women who cannot access community-based DV agencies or shelters are needed (Molina, Lawrence, & Azhar-Miller, 2009; Morales-Campos, Casillas & McCurdy 2009).[23] Often, immigrant Latina women cannot access programs in community-based DV shelters due to language barriers, fear of deportation, or difficulties with separating from their family members

(Brabeck, & Guzmán, 2009; Klevens et al., 2007).[24] The rapid growth of the Latino population within the United States necessitates an understanding of methods to decrease DV among this group.

Programs in community-based agencies

The majority of intervention efforts for women experiencing DV-related incidences with partners include empowering women through cognitive-behavioral changes to end a DV relationship (Allen & Wozniak, 2011; McPhail et al., 2007; Stover, Rainey, Berkman & Marans, 2008; Zust, 2006),[25] known as *crisis interventions* (i.e., education on navigating the criminal justice system); safety planning; short-term counseling at women's shelters; and support groups in community-based DV shelters or agencies (Allen & Wozniak, 2011; McPhail et al., 2007; Stover et al., 2008; Zust, 2006). Support groups conducted in community-based DV shelters or agencies use a specific educational curriculum to help women recover from a DV incident and increase self-esteem.

Programs outside of community-based DV shelters with specific curriculums exist but are rare. For example, Allen and Wozniak (2011)[26] examined a 10-week group intervention model called *Rites of Passage,* which uses a holistic and integrative curriculum focusing on women's self-development through stories, meditation, art therapy, self-reflection, and spiritual exercises. Using the Post-Traumatic Checklist as a pre- and posttest measure to assess the groups' effectiveness, findings indicated a reduction in posttraumatic stress symptoms, and themes of recovery (i.e., establishing autonomy and developing inner peace) emerged. Zust (2006)[27] used a phenomenological approach in a 20-week cognitive therapy program called INSIGHT (i.e., women learn positive thinking patterns that affect their perception of self). Findings indicated the women gained a deeper understanding of the self, and self-esteem increased, influencing their ability to develop goals free of violence.

Intervention programs for immigrant Latina women

One of few group-format programs designed to help immigrant Latinas understand DV within a cultural framework, Caminar Latino, Inc., uses ecological theory (i.e., understanding how environmental factors within larger systems influence romantic-relationship dynamics), feminist theory (i.e., understanding how power differentials between genders rooted in a patriarchal social system is the main cause of DV in society), and critical consciousness (i.e., an individual's ability to examine how society and culture influence his or her self-image) as foundations in providing the intervention (Perilla, Serrata, Weinberg, & Lippy, 2012).[28] Although the Caminar Latino, Inc. program is one intervention program specifically crafted with immigrant Latina women in mind, it is largely conducted in community-based DV shelters and agencies only. Thus it is important to develop more structured programs and curricula, which should be evaluated to assess their effectiveness, that can be used outside of community-based DV shelters or agencies. The SYP curriculum has undergone rigorous qualitative evaluation of the participants' experiences with the program and is receiving positive results.

Despite the lack of structured step-by step educational programs for immigrant Latinas, other community-based agencies programmatically addressing DV have been established in the United States, such as the National Latin@ Network (NLN) in Minneapolis/St. Paul, Minnesota. The NLN is a national project situated in *Casa de Esperanza* (i.e., shelter for immigrant Latina women) that focuses on DV within Latino communities (National Latin@ Network, 2015).[29] The NLN provides advocacy, resources, leadership development, training, and community engagement opportunities to Latinas and Latino families. Researchers, advocates, and staff at NLN engage in state and federal policy advocacy to work toward ending DV among Latino families. In addition, the NLN provides training and consultation to DV-related programs and services (e.g., shelters) in community-based agencies in the United States and Latin America and conducts ongoing, culturally relevant research to increase social awareness of DV among Latino communities (National Latin@ Network, 2015).

The NLN also provides psycho-educational support groups to Latina women. Because the NLN project is not situated in a mental health setting with mental health practitioners who are experienced in individual and group therapy, a structured program such as the SYP curriculum might be useful in this type of setting. This is an example in which the SYP curriculum might be beneficial in DV-related shelters and community-based agencies locally and nationally.

Other specific curricula (e.g., support-group format in DV shelters or community-based agencies) are available for Latina women in the general population, but limited availability exists for immigrant Latina women (Molina et al., 2009; Morales-Campos et al., 2009).[30] For example, Morales-Campos et al. (2009)[31] conducted interviews with 30 Latina participants exposed to DV incidences in current relationships to examine the benefits of a Spanish-speaking support group: Women learned how to manage feelings and DV-prone partners in relationships and examined ways to become more self-sufficient. The need to develop culturally competent curriculums and programs outside of community-based DV shelters or agencies for immigrant Latina women is important because it will increase availability and access to immigrant Latina women who may be experiencing DV.

NOTES

1. Edelson, M. G., Hokoda, A., & Ramos-Lira, L. (2007). Differences in effects of domestic violence between Latina and non-Latina women. *Journal of Family Violence, 22,* 1–10. doi:10.1007/s10896-006-9051-1; Hancock, T. (2007a). Addressing wife abuse in Mexican immigrant couples: Challenges for family social workers. *Journal of Family Social Work, 10,* 31–50. doi:10.1300/J039v10n03_03; Hancock, T. (2007b). Sin papeles: Undocumented Mexicans in rural United States. *Affilia: Journal of Women and Social Work, 22,* 175–184. doi:10.1177/0886109906299048; Hancock, T. U., & Ames, N. (2008). Toward a model for engaging Latino lay ministers in domestic violence intervention. *Families in Society: The Journal of Contemporary Social Services, 89,* 623–630. doi:10.1606/1044-3894.3824; Kasturirangan, A., Krishnan, S., & Riger, S. (2004). The impact of culture and minority status on women's experience of domestic violence. *Trauma, Violence, and Abuse, 5,* 318–332. doi: 10.1177/1524838004269487; Perilla, J. L. (1999). Domestic violence as a human rights issue: The case of immigrant Latinos. *Hispanic Journal of Behavioral Sciences, 21,* 107–133. doi:10.1177/0739986399212001; Vidales, G. T. (2010). Arrested justice: The multifaceted plight of immigrant Latinas who faced domestic violence. *Journal of Family Violence, 25,* 533–544. doi:10.1007/s10896-010-93095
2. Black, M. C., Basile, K. C., Breiding, M. J., Smith, S. G., Walters, M. L., Merrick, M. T., Chen, J., & Stevens, M. R. (2011). *The National Intimate Partner and Sexual Violence Survey (NISVS): 2010 Summary Report.* Atlanta, GA: National Center for Injury Prevention and Control, Centers for Disease Control and Prevention.
3. Black, M. C., Basile, K. C., Breiding, M. J., Smith, S. G., Walters, M. L., Merrick, M. T., Chen, J., & Stevens, M. R. (2011). *The National Intimate Partner and Sexual Violence Survey*

(NISVS): 2010 Summary Report. Atlanta, GA: National Center for Injury Prevention and Control, Centers for Disease Control and Prevention.

4. Brabeck, K. M., & Guzmán, M. R. (2009). Exploring Mexican-origin intimate partner abuse survivors' help-seeking within their sociocultural contexts. *Violence and Victims, 24*, 817–832. doi:10.1891/0886-6708.24.6.817; Kasturirangan, A., Krishnan, S., & Riger, S. (2004). The impact of culture and minority status on women's experience of domestic violence. *Trauma, Violence, and Abuse, 5*, 318–332. doi:10.1177/1524838004269487; Klevens, J., Shelley, G., Clavel-Arcas, C., Barney, D. D., Tobar, C., Duran, E. S., Barajas-Mazaheri, R., & Esparza, J. (2007). Latinos' perspectives and experiences with intimate partner violence. *Violence Against Women, 13*, 141–158. doi:10.1177/1077801206296980

   Vidales, G. T. (2010). Arrested justice: The multifaceted plight of immigrant Latinas who faced domestic violence. *Journal of Family Violence, 25*, 533–544. doi:10.1007/s10896-010-93095

5. Edelson, M. G., Hokoda, A., & Ramos-Lira, L. (2007). Differences in effects of domestic violence between Latina and non-Latina women. *Journal of Family Violence, 22*, 1–10. doi:10.1007/s10896-006-9051-1; Frias, S. M., & Angel, R. J. (2005). The risk of partner violence among low-income Hispanic subgroups. *Journal of Marriage and Family, 67*, 552–564. doi:10.1111/j.1741-3737.2005.00153.x; Hancock, T. (2007a). Addressing wife abuse in Mexican immigrant couples: Challenges for family social workers. *Journal of Family Social Work, 10*, 31–50. doi:10.1300/J039v10n03_03

6. Klevens, J. (2007). An overview of intimate partner violence among Latinos. *Violence Against Women, 13*, 111–122. doi:10.1177/1077801206296979

7. Brabeck, K. M., & Guzmán, M. R. (2009). Exploring Mexican-origin intimate partner abuse survivors' help-seeking within their sociocultural contexts. *Violence and Victims, 24*, 817–832. doi:10.1891/0886-6708.24.6.817

   Frias, S. M., & Angel, R. J. (2005). The risk of partner violence among low-income Hispanic subgroups. *Journal of Marriage and Family, 67*, 552–564. doi:10.1111/j.1741-3737.2005.00153.x; Vidales, G. T. (2010). Arrested justice: The multifaceted plight of immigrant Latinas who faced domestic violence. *Journal of Family Violence, 25*, 533–544. doi:10.1007/s10896-010-93095

8. Brabeck, K. M., & Guzmán, M. R. (2009). Exploring Mexican-origin intimate partner abuse survivors' help-seeking within their sociocultural contexts. *Violence and Victims, 24*, 817–832. doi:10.1891/0886-6708.24.6.817; Brabeck, K. M., & Guzman, M. R. (2008). Frequency and perceived effectiveness of strategies to survive abuse employed by battered Mexican-origin women. *Violence Against Women, 14*, 1274–1294. doi:10.1177/1077801208325087; Edelson, M. G., Hokoda, A., & Ramos-Lira, L. (2007). Differences in effects of domestic violence between Latina and Non-Latina women. *Journal of Family Violence, 22*, 1–10. doi:10.1007/s10896-006-9051-1; Klevens, J. (2007). An overview of intimate partner violence among Latinos. *Violence Against Women, 13*, 111–122. doi:10.1177/1077801206296979

9. Brabeck, K. M., & Guzmán, M. R. (2009). Exploring Mexican-origin intimate partner abuse survivors' help-seeking within their sociocultural contexts. *Violence and Victims, 24*, 817–832. doi:10.1891/0886-6708.24.6.817

10. Hancock, T. (2007a). Addressing wife abuse in Mexican immigrant couples: Challenges for family social workers. *Journal of Family Social Work, 10*, 31–50. doi:10.1300/J039v10n03_03; Vidales, G. T. (2010). Arrested justice: The multifaceted plight of immigrant Latinas who faced domestic violence. *Journal of Family Violence, 25*, 533–544. doi:10.1007/s10896-010-93095

11. Reina, A. S., Lohman, B. J., & Maldonado, M. M. (2014). "He said they'd deport me": Factors influencing domestic violence help-seeking practices among Latina immigrants. *Journal of Interpersonal Violence, 29*(4), 593–615. doi:10.1177/0886260513505214; Sabina, C., Cuevas, C. A., & Schally, J. L. (2012). Help-seeking in a national sample of victimized Latino women: The influence of victimization types. *Journal of Interpersonal Violence, 27*, 40–61. doi:10.1177/0886260511416460

12. Sabina, C., Cuevas, C. A., & Schally, J. L. (2012). Help-seeking in a national sample of victimized Latino women: The influence of victimization types. *Journal of Interpersonal Violence, 27*, 40–61. doi:10.1177/0886260511416460

13. Goldman, M. (1999). The violence against women act: Meeting its goals in protecting battered immigrant women? *Family and Conciliation Courts Review, 37,* 375–392. doi:10.1111/j.174-1617.1999.tb01311.x; Parmley, A. M. (2004). Violence against women research post VAWA, where have we been, where are we going? *Violence against Women, 10,* 1417–1430. doi:10.1177/1077801204270682; U.S. Department of Justice. (2015). *Application for cancellation of removal and adjustment of status for certain nonpermanent residents.* Retrieved October 29, 2015, from Executive Office for Immigration Review: http://www.justice.gov/sites/default/files/pages/attachments/2015/07/24/eoir42b.pdf

14. Goldman, M. (1999). The Violence Against Women Act: Meeting its goals in protecting battered immigrant women? *Family and Conciliation Courts Review, 37,* 375–392. doi:10.1111/j.174-1617.1999.tb01311.x; Parmley, A. M. (2004). Violence against women research post VAWA: Where have we been, where are we going? *Violence against Women, 10,* 1417–1430. doi:10.1177/1077801204270682

15. Broder, T. (2005). Immigrant eligibility for public benefits. In *Immigration & Nationality Law Handbook* (pp. 759–782). Washington, DC: American Immigration Lawyers Association.

16. U.S. Department of Justice. (2015). *Application for cancellation of removal and adjustment of status for certain nonpermanent residents.* Retrieved October 29, 2015, from Executive Office for Immigration Review: http://www.justice.gov/sites/default/files/pages/attachments/2015/07/24/eoir42b.pdf

17. Broder, T. (2005). Immigrant eligibility for public benefits. In *Immigration & Nationality Law Handbook* (pp. 759–782). Washington, DC: American Immigration Lawyers Association; Legal Momentum Advancing Women's Rights. (2005). *Public benefits access for battered immigrant women and children.* Retrieved from National Online Resource Center on Violence Against Women: http://www.vawnet.org/summary.php?doc_id=1605&find_type=web_sum_GC

18. Furman, R., & Negi, N. J. (2007). Social work practice with transnational Latino populations. *International Social Work, 50*(1), 107–112. doi:10.1177/0020872807072500

19. Alcalde, M. C. (2010). Violence across borders: Familism, hegemonic masculinity, and self-sacrificing femininity in the lives of Mexican and Peruvian migrant. *Latino Studies, 8*(1), 48–68. doi:10.1057/lst.2009.44; Domínguez, S., & Lubitow, A. (2008). Transnational ties, poverty, and identity: Latin American immigrant women in public housing. *Family Relations, 57*(4), 419–430. Retrieved from http://www.jstor.org.ezproxy.stthomas.edu/stable/20456807; Furman, R., & Negi, N. J. (2007). Social work practice with transnational Latino populations. *International Social Work, 50*(1), 107–112. doi:10.1177/0020872807072500

20. Domínguez, S., & Lubitow, A. (2008). Transnational ties, poverty, and identity: Latin American immigrant women in public housing. *Family Relations, 57*(4), 419–430. Retrieved from http://www.jstor.org.ezproxy.stthomas.edu/stable/20456807

21. Alcalde, M. C. (2010). Violence across borders: Familism, hegemonic masculinity, and self-sacrificing femininity in the lives of Mexican and Peruvian migrant. *Latino Studies, 8*(1), 48–68. doi:10.1057/lst.2009.44

22. Allen, K. N., & Wozniak, D. F. (2011). The language of healing: Women's voices in healing and recovering from domestic violence. *Social Work in Mental Health, 9,* 37–55. doi:10.1080/15332985.2010.494540; McPhail, B. A., Busch, N. B., Kulkarni, S., & Rice, G. (2007). An integrative feminist model: The evolving feminist perspective on intimate partner violence. *Violence Against Women, 13,* 817–841. doi:10.1177/1077801207302039; Whitaker, D. J., Baker, C. K., Pratt, C., Reed, E., Suri, S., Pavlos, C., Nagy, B. J., & Silverman, J. (2007). A network model for providing culturally competent services for partner violence and sexual violence. *Violence Against Women, 13,* 190–209. doi:10.1177/1077801206296984

23. Molina, O., Lawrence, S. A., & Azhar-Miller, A. (2009). Divorcing abused Latina immigrant women's experiences with domestic violence support groups. *Journal of Divorce and Remarriage, 50,* 459–471. doi:10.1080/10502550902970561; Morales-Campos, D. Y., Casillas, M., & McCurdy, S. A. (2009). From isolation to connection: Understanding a support group for Hispanic women living with gender-based violence in Houston, Texas. *Journal of Immigrant Minority Health, 11,* 57–65. doi:10.1007/s10903-008-9153-3.

24. Brabeck, K. M., & Guzmán, M. R. (2009). Exploring Mexican-origin intimate partner abuse survivors' help-seeking within their sociocultural contexts. *Violence and Victims, 24,* 817–832.

doi:10.1891/0886-6708.24.6.817; Klevens, J., Shelley, G., Clavel-Arcas, C., Barney, D. D., Tobar, C., Duran, E. S., Barajas-Mazaheri, R., & Esparza, J. (2007). Latinos' perspectives and experiences with intimate partner violence. *Violence Against Women, 13*, 141–158. doi:10.1177/1077801206296980

25. Allen, K. N., & Wozniak, D. F. (2011). The language of healing: Women's voices in healing and recovering from domestic violence. *Social Work in Mental Health, 9*, 37–55. doi:10.1080/15332985.2010.494540; McPhail, B. A., Busch, N. B., Kulkarni, S., & Rice, G. (2007). An integrative feminist model: The evolving feminist perspective on intimate partner violence. *Violence Against Women, 13*, 817–841. doi:10.1177/1077801207302039; Stover, C. S., Rainey, A. M., Berkman, M., & Marans, S. (2008). Factors associated with engagement in a police-advocacy home-visit intervention to prevent domestic violence. *Violence Against Women, 14*, 1430–1450. doi:1177/1077801208327019; Zust, B. L. (2006). Meaning of INSIGHT participation among women who have experienced intimate partner violence. *Issues in Mental Health Nursing, 27*, 775–793. doi:10.1080/01612840600781170

26. Allen, K. N., & Wozniak, D. F. (2011). The language of healing: Women's voices in healing and recovering from domestic violence. *Social Work in Mental Health, 9*, 37–55. doi:10.1080/15332985.2010.494540

27. Zust, B. L. (2006). Meaning of INSIGHT participation among women who have experienced intimate partner violence. *Issues in Mental Health Nursing, 27*, 775–793. doi:10.1080/01612840600781170

28. Perilla, J. L., Serrata, J. V., Weinberg, J. & Lippy, C. (2012). Integrating women's voices and theory: A comprehensive domestic violence intervention for Latinas. *Women and Therapy, 35*, 93–105. doi:10.1080/02703149.2012.634731

29. National Latin@ Network. (n.d.). Retrieved October 28, 2015, from National Latin@ Network: http://www.nationallatinonetwork.org/

30. Molina, O., Lawrence, S. A., & Azhar-Miller, A. (2009). Divorcing abused Latina immigrant women's experiences with domestic violence support groups. *Journal of Divorce and Remarriage, 50*, 459–471. doi:10.1080/10502550902970561; Morales-Campos, D. Y., Casillas, M., & McCurdy, S. A. (2009). From isolation to connection: Understanding a support group for Hispanic women living with gender-based violence in Houston, Texas. *Journal of Immigrant Minority Health, 11*, 57–65. doi:10.1007/s10903-008-9153-3.

31. Morales-Campos, D. Y., Casillas, M., & McCurdy, S. A. (2009). From isolation to connection: Understanding a support group for Hispanic women living with gender-based violence in Houston, Texas. *Journal of Immigrant Minority Health, 11*, 57–65. doi:10.1007/s10903-008-9153-3.

3

THEORETICAL BACKGROUND

SEVERAL SOCIOLOGICAL, SOCIAL WORK, AND THERAPEUTIC THEORIES were utilized in the formation, development, revision, and process of creating the *Sí, Yo Puedo* (SYP) program. These included (a) *intersectionality* (i.e., examining the intersection of concepts such as immigration status, domestic violence (DV), race/ethnicity, and culture); (b) *feminist ideology* (i.e., examining power differences between genders and a patriarchal system); (c) *group theory* (i.e., knowledge of the group facilitator's role and group work and dynamics); and (d) the *domestic violence empowerment framework* (i.e., raising awareness and providing education). The primary theory that guided the development of the SYP program manual was intersectionality (Bhuyan & Velagapudi, 2013; Messing, Becerra, Ward-Lasher, & Androff, 2015; Reina, Lohman, & Maldonado, 2014).[1]

INTERSECTIONALITY

Intersectionality is conceptualized as the crossroads between forms or systems of oppression, domination, or discrimination, such as gender, race/ethnicity, class, or sexual orientation (Bhuyan & Velagapudi, 2013; Messing et al., 2015; Reina et al., 2014)[2] and was a helpful conceptual framework in the development of the SYP curriculum and program. Because this perspective is commonly associated with feminist theory and feminists of color, it was important to examine my own intersecting identities and position. I am a first-generation privileged immigrant Latina woman who was born in Lima, Peru, and who has predominantly lived in the United States. I speak fluent Spanish and understand Latino cultural norms and values, and I have worked with immigrant Latina women (i.e., mostly from Mexico) who have experienced incidences of DV as a licensed clinical social worker for several decades. My intersecting identities and position influenced my understanding of immigrant Latinas who experienced incidences of DV and oppression related to immigration and citizenship status and access to resources and types of support (Erez, Adelman, & Gregory, 2009).[3]

In addition to discrimination resulting from gender and race/ethnicity, discrimination in the forms of immigration status, language barriers, and socioeconomic status (e.g., minimal access to education) likely comprise the multiple identities and lived experiences of immigrant Latina women who might be experiencing incidences of DV and who want to improve current romantic relationships (Bhuyan & Velagapudi, 2013; Reina et al., 2014).[4] Feminists of color in Latina/ Chicana studies, such as Gloria Anzaldúa, examines the challenges of Mexican immigrant Latina women living between physical borders (i.e., the United States and Mexico) in relation to race, gender, and class (Campbell, 2008; González-López, 2007).[5] The changing of gender roles might create more opportunities and at the same time might cause tension within the family unit, especially when a victim of DV is trying to access resources and support systems. Other Latina scholars have addressed the intersection between sexual violence and gender and migration experiences (González-López, 2007).[6] For example, González-López

(2007)[7] discussed the importance of understanding how the multiple intersections of immigrant Latinas impact help-seeking behaviors, family support, and current relationships. By incorporating intersectionality as a conceptual framework, researchers and practitioners can gain a better understanding of the unique needs of immigrant Latina women and apply a culturally competent group intervention in the SYP program. Other important DV conceptual frameworks, such as feminist ideology and the family violence perspective, guided the development of the SYP curriculum and program.

FEMINIST IDEOLOGY: CAUSES OF DOMESTIC VIOLENCE

Feminist ideology examines the power differences between men and women within a patriarchal society. According to feminist ideology, DV occurs within the context of a male–female relationship in which abuse is a man's attempt to reassert gender differences and gender dominance (Perilla, Frndak, Lillard, & East, 2003).[8] Women's roles and men's roles are defined in society, and a division of labor and responsibilities of work within and outside the home adds to the power imbalance within the male–female relationship. Perilla et al. (2003)[9] explained how the imbalance within the male–female relationship promotes acts of DV: Men are violent toward women because they want to control them. Feminist ideology is the dominant theory that explains DV, and the majority of service providers are trained under feminist ideology.

FAMILY VIOLENCE PERSPECTIVE

Other ideological theories inform understanding, research, treatment, and support for those experiencing DV. The family violence perspective suggests that abuse is a problem that occurs within the family, and all family members are victims of violence (Walker, 2002).[10] According to this theoretical framework, the structure of the family in the United States is affected by societal stressors, which allow for family members to use violence against one another (Kurz, 1989).[11] In addition, abusive behavior is modeled for males in their family of origin, and women and men engage in equal amounts of violence (Kurz, 1989).[12]

SOCIAL WORK AND THERAPEUTIC THEORIES

In conjunction with an intersectionality lens, several therapeutic theories have guided group facilitation and dynamics for mental health professionals. First, social work theories that address immigrant Latina women's strengths, resiliency, and empowerment have been used within a cultural framework. For SYP the strengths perspective was used to draw on immigrant Latina's women's strengths (e.g., the ability to maintain their family intact despite DV incidences) within the context of the family (Saleebey, 1996).[13] Second, cognitive behavioral theory (i.e., the examination of automatic thoughts and the impact of thoughts on emotions and behavior; Beck, 2011)[14] and attachment theory (i.e., examining early childhood attachment patterns with caregivers and the impact of those attachments in adult functioning; Bowlby, 1988)[15] were used to integrate topics such as coping strategies and influences of past traumas.

Group theory

Group theory incorporates an understanding of group dynamics, facilitator role, and managing groups (Toseland & Rivas, 2017).[16] Group theory guided mental health professionals in facilitating the groups, especially as group facilitators vacillated between the teacher role and the facilitative role (Lieberman & Golant, 2002; Robbins, Tonemah, & Robbins, 2002; Toseland & Rivas, 2017).[17] Although the group worker role was predominantly that of teacher (i.e., specific content was taught each week), the group worker leader also provided a facilitative role that contributed to the participants' overall experience (Robbins, et al., 2002; Toseland & Rivas, 2017).[18] Group facilitators used group theory and techniques as they facilitated the weekly topics in the SYP program.

Domestic violence empowerment framework

An important DV framework was used throughout the SYP curriculum. The psycho-educational and empowerment counseling framework with a focus on advocacy (i.e., providing education on DV such as legal resources and access to those resources, providing options for women experiencing DV, and empowering women to examine current relationships; Pence, 2001; Walker, 2002)[19] informed topics of dating, healthy relationships, and DV. Finally, community-based participatory research was used to conduct the evaluation of the SYP curriculum program manual. Community-based participatory research involves working with community agencies to conduct research projects that meet the needs of clients (Ahmed, Beck, Maurana, & Newton, 2004).[20]

NOTES

1. Bhuyan, R., & Velagapudi, K. (2013). From one "Dragon Sleigh" to another: Advocating for immigrant women facing violence in Kansas. *Affilia: Journal of Women and Social Work, 28*, 65–78. doi:10.1177/0886109912475049; Messing, J. T., Becerra, D., Ward-Lasher, A. & Androff, D. K. (2015). Latinas' perceptions of law enforcement: Fear of deportation, crime reporting, and trust in the system. *Affilia: Journal of Women and Social Work, 1–13.* doi:10.1177/0886109915576520; Reina, A. S., Lohman, B. J., & Maldonado, M. M. (2014). "He said they'd deport me": Factors influencing domestic violence help-seeking practices among Latina immigrants. *Journal of Interpersonal Violence, 29*(4), 593–615. doi:10.1177/ 0886260513505214

2. Bhuyan, R., & Velagapudi, K. (2013). From one "Dragon Sleigh" to another: Advocating for immigrant women facing violence in Kansas. *Affilia: Journal of Women and Social Work, 28*, 65–78. doi:10.1177/0886109912475049; Messing, J. T., Becerra, D., Ward-Lasher, A. & Androff, D. K. (2015). Latinas' perceptions of law enforcement: Fear of deportation, crime reporting, and trust in the system. *Affilia: Journal of Women and Social Work, 1–13.* doi:10.1177/0886109915576520; Reina, A. S., Lohman, B. J., & Maldonado, M. M. (2014). "He said they'd deport me": Factors influencing domestic violence help-seeking practices among Latina immigrants. *Journal of Interpersonal Violence, 29*(4), 593–615. doi:10.1177/ 0886260513505214

3. Erez, E., Adelman, M., & Gregory, C. (2009). Intersections of immigration and domestic violence: Voices of battered immigrant women. *Feminist Criminology, 4*, 32–56. doi:10.1177/ 1557085108325413

4. Bhuyan, R., & Velagapudi, K. (2013). From one "Dragon Sleigh" to another: Advocating for immigrant women facing violence in Kansas. *Affilia: Journal of Women and Social Work, 28*, 65–78. doi 10.1177/0886109912475049; Reina, A. S., Lohman, B. J., & Maldonado, M. M. (2014). "He said they'd deport me": Factors influencing domestic violence help-seeking practices among Latina immigrants. *Journal of Interpersonal Violence, 29*(4), 593–615. doi:10.1177/0886260513505214

5. Campbell, W. S. (2008). Lessons in resilience: Undocumented Mexican women in South Carolina. *Affilia: Journal of Women and Social Work, 23*, 231–241. doi:10.1177/ 0886109908319172; González-López, G. (2007). "Nunca he dejado de tener terror": Sexual violence in the lives of Mexican immigrant women. In D. A. Segura & P. Zavella (Eds.), *Women*

and migration in the U.S.-Mexico borderlands: A reader (pp. 224–246). Durham, NC: Duke University Press.

6. González-López, G. (2007). "Nunca he dejado de tener terror": Sexual violence in the lives of Mexican immigrant women. In D. A. Segura & P. Zavella (Eds.), *Women and migration in the U.S.-Mexico borderlands: A reader* (pp. 224–246). Durham, NC: Duke University Press.

7. Ibid.

8. Perilla, J. L., Frndak, K., Lillard, D., & East, C. (2003). A working analysis of women's use of violence in the context of learning, opportunity, and choice. *Violence Against Women, 9,* 10–46.

9. Ibid.

10. Walker, L. E. (2002). The politics of trauma practice: Politics, psychology and the battered woman's movement. *Journal of Trauma Practice, 1,* 81–102.

11. Kurz, D. (1989). Social science perspectives on wife abuse: Current debates and future directions. *Gender & Society, 3,* 489–505.

12. Ibid.

13. Saleebey, D. (1996). The strengths perspective in social work practice: Extensions and cautions. *Social Work, 3,* 296–305.

14. Beck, J. S. (2011). *Cognitive therapy: Basics and beyond* (2nd ed.) New York: Guilford Press.

15. Bowlby, J. (1988). Developmental psychiatry comes of age. *The American Journal of Psychiatry, 1,* 1–9.

16. Toseland, R. W., & Rivas, R. F. (2017). *An introduction to group work practice: Connecting core competencies series* (8th ed.). Boston, MA: Pearson Education.

17. Lieberman, M., & Golant, M. (2002). Leader behaviors as perceived by cancer patients in professionally directed support groups and outcomes. *Group Dynamics: Theory, Research, and Practice, 6,* 267–276. doi:10.1037//1089-2699.6.4.267; Robbins, R., Tonemah, S., & Robbins, S. (2002). Project eagle: Techniques for multi-family psycho-educational group. *American Indian and Alaska Native Mental Health Research, 10,* 56–74. doi:10.5820/aian.1003.2002.56; Toseland, R. W., & Rivas, R. F. (2017). *An introduction to group work practice: Connecting core competencies series* (8th ed.). Boston, MA: Pearson Education.

18. Robbins, R., Tonemah, S., & Robbins, S. (2002). Project eagle: Techniques for multi-family psycho-educational group. *American Indian and Alaska Native Mental Health Research, 10,* 56–74. doi:10.5820/aian.1003.2002.56; Toseland, R. W., & Rivas, R. F. (2017). *An introduction to group work practice: Connecting core competencies series* (8th ed.). Boston, MA: Pearson Education.

19. Pence, E. (2001). Advocacy on behalf of battered women. In C. M. Renzetti, J. L. Edleson, & R. K. Bergen (Eds.), *Sourcebook on violence against women* (pp. 329–343). Thousand Oaks, CA: SAGE; Walker, L. E. (2002). The politics of trauma practice: Politics, psychology and the battered woman's movement. *Journal of Trauma Practice, 1,* 81–102.

20. Ahmed, S. M., Beck, B, Maurana, C. A, & Newton, G. (2004). Overcoming barriers to effective community-based participatory research in U.S. medical schools. *Education for Health, 17*(2), 141–151. doi:10.1080/13576280410001710969

4 GROUP FORMAT AND GROUP WORK

LICENSED MENTAL HEALTH PROFESSIONALS AS FACILITATORS AND CULTURAL AWARENESS

Facilitators of the *Sí, Yo Puedo* (SYP) program must be licensed mental health professionals with graduate degrees who come from various mental health backgrounds and who have experience with facilitating groups. For example, facilitators might be licensed independent clinical social workers (LICSW), licensed certified social workers (LCSW), licensed professional counselors (LPC), licensed family and marriage therapists (LMFT), licensed psychologists, and psychiatrists (MD). Facilitators must have proficient Spanish-speaking writing, reading, and speaking ability, as the groups are purposefully conducted in Spanish. For example, a facilitator must be able to easily converse with participants in the groups and assess any mental health concern or crisis that might occur in the groups. Facilitators with a Latino cultural background and who identify as being part of the Latino culture might have a better understanding of the cultural dynamics; however, non-Latino facilitators who do not identify as being part of the Latino culture may also facilitate the groups. Facilitators should have an understanding of the cultural influences of *familism, machismo,* and *marianismo* on women's experiences with dating and current relationships. The psycho-educational groups can be co-facilitated (two facilitators) or can be individually facilitated. Whether to co-facilitate or individually facilitate the groups will be decided by the agency program supervisors and mental health professionals.

TEACHING AND INSTRUCTIONAL METHODS

Several teaching strategies (i.e., teaching specific content material, large-group discussion, self-reflection writing and drawing activities, and teaching relaxation exercises to manage problems) are used in the sessions. Each session begins with a reflection exercise to help participants begin the process of self-awareness about each topic. Table 4.1 depicts the types of self-reflection drawing and writing exercises. Participants share their reflection exercises if they wish to do so and often large-group discussion occurs. The facilitator teaches on specific content in each of the sessions and at the same time encourages participants to share their experiences with group members. Participants also engage in self-reflection exercises in interims between classes. For example, in the class on healthy relationships, one of the self-reflection exercises involves answering the following question: "How do I view my relationship? Are there positive or negative characteristics in my relationship?" Participants support and learn from one another as they share their self-reflective exercises.

An assumption in utilizing the SYP curriculum is that mental health professionals will have knowledge and experience in facilitating groups in direct practice

Table 4.1 INTRODUCTION

SYP CURRICULUM AND WEEKLY TOPICS

		Large Group Discussion	Instruction/Psycho-Education: Teach on Topics	Self-Reflection Drawing or Writing Activity
Part I: Awareness of Self	*Week 1: Introductions Who am I?*	Identity and awareness of self.	Values and beliefs.	Who am I folder activity.
	Week 2: Coping strategies	Coping strategies.	Definition of coping and positive and negative coping strategies. Relaxation and deep breath exercises.	Identify four problems and how coping strategies.
	Week 3: Self-esteem	Identify self-esteem.	Definition of self-esteem and assessment of current self-esteem.	What do I think and feel about myself.
	Week 4: Influences of past traumas	Influences of past traumas on women's sense of self.	Dynamics and definition of sexual abuse, child abuse, or other types of traumas as identified by the participants.	Time line activity.
Part II: Knowledge of Relationship within Culture	*Week 5: Dating*	Dynamics of dating experiences within the Latino culture.	Characteristics of healthy dating.	What does dating look like? Draw or write about your first dating experience.
	Week 6: Cultural concepts: Familism, Machismo and Marianismo	Cultural concepts and how that impacts participant's knowledge of dating and healthy relationships.	Knowledge of *familism, machismo* and *marianismo*.	Draw a picture or write about cultural concepts influencing relationships. Alternate: Genogram/ Identify Family Patterns.
	Week 7: Healthy Relationships	Healthy relationships.	Characteristics of healthy relationships; Use equality wheel handout; Healthy relationships characteristics handout.	Draw a picture of how I view my current relationship.
	Week 8: Domestic Violence	Domestic violence.	Dynamics, definition, types of abuse found in domestic violence, legal issues, and overall prevalence rates.	None

(Continued)

Table 4.1 (*cont.*)

		Large Group Discussion	Instruction/Psycho-Education: Teach on Topics	Self-Reflection Drawing or Writing Activity
Part III: Impact of Factors on Relationships	*Week 9: Factors Influencing Relationships*	Factors that influence women's understanding of relationships.	Specific factors such as the media, parents, and religious institutions.	Factors, are they positive or negative influences?
	Week 9: Alternate Topic: Sexual Abuse	Impact of childhood sexual abuse on adult relationships.	Definition of childhood sexual abuse, how to protect children (e.g., signs to look for), and how to access resources in the community.	None
	Week 10: Talking to Children	Women's ability to talk to their children (girls and boys) about healthy dating.	Sensitive topics such as healthy communication and relationships with their children and teenagers.	Draw a picture of a crystal ball and write a letter to your child. What will you say?
	Week 11: Resources and Graduation	Empowerment and changes.	Safety measures and mental health/ domestic violence resource handout.	Suitcase Activity, What will I take with me? Meal, graduation, presentation of certificate, group members exchange phone numbers.

[1] *Table created by author: Catherine Luz Marrs Fuchsel*

settings and are skilled in conducting diagnostic assessments and interventions using a specific treatment model. Mental health professionals most likely will have different experiences with facilitating groups and direct practice skills such as assessments and treatment planning; however, with master's degrees and licensure requirements for mental health professionals, it is assumed that most mental health professionals will have been exposed to some type of knowledge of group work and theory and assessments and interventions in their respective graduate programs and continuing education hours for maintaining licensure in their respective states.

The SYP curriculum relies heavily on group facilitators' ability to teach on specific content material in the weekly topics and have prior knowledge on each of the topics (e.g., coping skills, self-esteem, healthy relationships, cultural concepts, domestc violence [DV]). For those reasons, it is recommended that mental health professionals have prior knowledge in group work and an understanding of the teacher and facilitator role in conducting groups. The teacher role in facilitating educational groups is one of teaching specific content to group participants and processing and facilitating participants' experiences in the group. In addition, if mental health professionals lack knowledge in specific content that is covered in the weekly classes, such as relaxation exercises and deep breathing in Week 2, it is recommended that they participate in professional workshops via continuing education hours (i.e., a licensure requirement) to learn more about specific content. Last, a list of additional readings on content is available in each of the weekly classes that includes goals and objectives.

DUAL ROLE FOR FACILITATOR AND SELF-DISCLOSURE

The role of facilitator, or teacher, is an important component of psycho-educational groups (Lieberman & Golant, 2002; Robbins, et al., 2002; Toseland & Rivas, 2017).[1] Although the facilitator role is predominantly that of teacher (i.e., specific content is taught each week), this group leader also provides a facilitative role that contributes to the participants' overall experience (Robbins, et al., 2002; Toseland & Rivas, 2017).[2] For example, the facilitator provides a structured format setting in the group and offers problem-solving statements by asking empathic and open-ended questions, allowing for a dynamic interaction among group members and the facilitator. The facilitator oversees an environment in which group members take responsibility and action for the group process in a supportive and therapeutic space in which immigrant Latina women can disclose information.

Facilitators of the psycho-educational groups use their clinical skills to help participants understand healthy relationships. In addition, facilitators use self-disclosure as a method of modeling for immigrant Latina women their own experiences of healthy relationships and assessment of self-esteem. Self-disclosure is a practical and useful intervention when working with individuals in group settings. Oftentimes, mental health professionals will use self-disclosure that will benefit the client as an intervention tool. From a cultural perspective, the Latino culture embraces an open family unit (e.g., *familism*). Family members support one another, share a high sense of unity, and are very close in relationships. This phenomenon is carried over to other types of relationships, and facilitators might experience this unity and closeness in the participant–facilitator relationship. Self-disclosure in this context is embraced and welcomed by group facilitators. For those reasons, facilitators are encouraged to do the drawing and writing activities alongside participants at the beginning of each class. Facilitators can choose to share their own experiences with participants by sharing their drawing and writing activities.

GROUP PROCESS AND EMPOWERMENT

As immigrant Latina women learn new content each week and begin to experience group cohesion and collaboration (Toseland & Rivas, 2017),[3] they might start to ask more questions about dating, healthy relationships, and the dynamics of DV. As they learn new information and interact among each other, they report their self-esteem improves and they begin the process of becoming empowered.

Immigrant Latina women in groups experience the process of empowerment (i.e., the ability to become aware and conscious of self and environmental factors that influence an individual's ability to create change in the present or in the future; Kasturirangan, 2008)[4] as they share their stories and experience with the specific topics in each of the sessions. Immigrant Latina women might become empowered by learning from each other, supporting one another, listening to each other, and problem-solving together. As immigrant Latina women became more aware of self and partners, they may feel empowered to examine current relationships and dating experiences within their own culture, became more aware of their self-worth, feel more capable of making decisions about the type of relationships and families they want, and perhaps examine options to return to school or find work. Specifically, as immigrant Latina women's self-esteem increases and they became more aware of what they want, they begin to discuss future goals. This is important because women's increased self-esteem leads to the possibility of future decision-making abilities about what they want for themselves and their children outside of potentially or confirmed unsafe relationships (Marrs Fuchsel, 2014a; Marrs Fuchsel & Hysjulien, 2013).[5]

PHYSICAL ENVIRONMENT AND SETTING UP GROUPS

A complete description of the roles and responsibilities for facilitators is depicted in Table 4.2. The sponsoring social service agencies, community health clinics, faith-based programs, or other agencies using the SYP curriculum provide the space for the psycho-educational groups. It is recommended that the space provided (e.g., conference room or classroom at the agency, home nearby) includes a blackboard or a flip chart with markers and erasers so that facilitators can organize presentation of items, such as the agenda, group rules, reflection exercises for the session, and participants' responses. Rooms at the agency should include outlets, access to an Internet connection, chairs, and tables because participants write or draw reflection exercises at the beginning of each session. Facilitators should plan to have the following materials available for each of the weekly sessions:

- File folders (manila; one for each participant)
- Markers and pens
- Tape and scissors
- Stickers (stickers with happy faces, flowers, peace and love signs, anything that might emit positive thoughts)
- Radio, CD player, laptop computer, or digital device (to play relaxing background music while participants are writing or drawing)
- Paper (white or color) for the in-class reflection exercises

Groups typically range between 8 and 10 group members; however, the size of the group will vary based on recruitment efforts, geographic location, and agency and programmatic needs. The type of group format used is a closed-group format (i.e., no other participant will be allowed to participate in the group after the group begins). By providing a closed-group format, group members begin the process of trusting each other and building rapport; they begin to share their experiences and support one another as they disclose very personal stories.

Diversity in groups

Facilitators should be aware of the diversity among immigrant Latina women when they recruit participants and the impact of diversity in the groups. Immigrant Latina women participating in the psycho-educational groups will come from different Spanish-speaking countries (including the United States), with different life experiences and acculturation dynamics. Similarly, participating women will vary in age, educational level, relationship status, parenting status, legal status, English-language proficiency, and writing proficiency. In addition, some of the participants might be related or know each other from previous groups. For example, some of the participants might be mother/daughter or sister/sister-in-law related. Facilitators should discuss with participants prior to the group starting about the impact of participants knowing each other in the group experience. Diversity in groups will likely contribute to the group dynamics, including participants' level of learning and support for one another. It is important to note that some participants may not be able to read or write. Participants in the initial pilot study of the SYP curriculum who could not read or write felt more comfortable drawing self-reflection activities, and participants were reminded that drawing was just as valuable as reading and writing.

Being flexible in groups

Flexibility is an important concept to address when working with the SYP curriculum and group work. Facilitators should be flexible and understanding when

Table 4.2 FACILITATOR'S ROLES AND RESPONSIBILITY

Starting the Group	Facilitator's Responsibility	Facilitator Competency
Intake meeting	• Assess for homicidal and suicidal ideation • Assess for current domestic violence in relationships and possible safety planning • Assess for issues of mandated reporting and confidentiality • Assess for crisis situation • Knowledge and access to mental health/domestic violence resource handout	• Crisis intervention • Domestic violence empowerment framework/counseling; advocacy • Mandated reporting • Knowledge of community-based programs and resources in the community
Group materials	• File folders (manila folders) • Markers, pens, pencils • Stickers • Scissors • Tape • White or color paper • Radio, CD player, laptop computer, or digital device	
Set up room and location	• Private room in agency (e.g., a conference room with tables and chairs) • Rooms that include outlets and access to an Internet connection • Blackboard or flipchart to use for writing and drawing	
Arrange for childcare and food	• Organize childcare and food for childcare	

Table created by author.

working with immigrant Latina women who might be working, caring for a loved one, or raising a family. Often participants may miss, arrive late to, or leave early from a group session (or many group sessions). During the intake procedure, facilitators explain to the participants that they will benefit most from the SYP curriculum and program if they are able to attend every session because each topic builds upon the previous one; however, sometimes participants miss a session for unexpected reasons. Facilitators should be flexible and encourage participants to attend the next session.

Weekly topics build on previous ones, and sometimes the participants need more time to process and discuss the topic at hand. This dilemma usually occurs during Week 4 (i.e., session on past childhood traumas) as participants disclose information from their past. The facilitator will need to decide if another session on the same topic is necessary because of time restraints. Relatedly, participants may have an infant or small child they need to bring to the group if childcare is unavailable. Facilitators should similarly be flexible regarding family dynamics and separation issues with children. Whether older children—who could understand and potentially repeat disclosed information—are allowed to attend is at the discretion of the facilitator and other group participants.

Managing a crisis in groups

Facilitators should be competent in crisis intervention in a group setting when a crisis occurs. The participants in the group vary in the type of romantic relationships they might be experiencing and their overall mental and physical health. For example, some of the participants may be dating, legally married (e.g., civil or religious marriage), cohabituating, or single. Some participants might be in a DV or non-DV relationship. For example, one participant who was experiencing DV in her relationship disclosed that her husband had physically assaulted her in the fifth session of the program. The participant described a fight that escalated into a physical assault in the home between Weeks 4 and 5 (i.e., research project examining immigrant Mexican women's experiences with the SYP curriculum; Marrs Fuchsel & Hysjulien, 2013).[6] In this situation, the group facilitator and support staff met with the participant and provided a safety plan that included legal resources, information on accessing the police department, and counseling services in local mental health agencies. Thus facilitators must be knowledgeable about crisis intervention for DV situations. The use of clinical skills is important in managing a crisis in the group.

Participants who take part in the SYP program may not necessarily be in a DV-related relationship; however, findings from the current research project indicated several participants' disclosure of being in a relationship that involved DV (Marrs Fuchsel & Hysjulien, 2013).[7] Participants who disclosed being in a DV-related relationship might be exposed to greater risk of escalation of violence due to their partner's controlling tendencies. Another important consideration is participants' experiencing the process of empowerment. As immigrant Latina women learn more about healthy relationships and DV, they might confront their partners and disrupt family harmony, putting them at greater risk.

Other sensitive topics, such as past traumas, expose participants to information that might be difficult to process in psycho-educational groups. On several occasions, participants disclosed a past trauma (e.g., past DV incidences or childhood sexual abuse) for the first time in a group session, and this type of exposure might trigger a traumatic memory or event (Marrs Fuchsel et al., 2015).[8] For those reasons, it is crucial that mental health practitioners facilitating the groups have knowledge and understanding of DV crises situations. Mental health practitioners should have knowledge of the domestic violence empowerment framework, know how to help a participant make a safety plan, and have access to resources, such as DV advocates in local police departments, counseling services in community-based agencies, shelters, and crisis hotlines in their respective communities. Finally, group facilitators managing sensitive topics in the weekly sessions must use their therapeutic crisis skills and empowerment counseling framework to assist the participants with safety planning, access to resources, support systems, and offering immediate solutions and additional individual counseling services.

STARTING THE GROUP

Intake process for immigrant Latina women

Initial intake meetings are conducted to discuss the SYP curriculum and psycho-educational group program, obtain consent and demographic information, review issues of confidentiality, and assess for safety in current relationships. Demographic information is collected for the purposes of understanding group diversity for use among group facilitators. The social service agencies provide the intake and assessment forms. During the initial intake meeting, facilitators also assess for current suicidal or homicidal ideation. Participants who disclose current suicidal or homicidal ideation should not be included in the program because it is beyond the scope of the psycho-educational group format. Participants who disclose current suicidal or homicidal ideation should be assessed and the proper level of care should be provided (i.e., crisis intervention, hospitalization, or individual therapy). Immigrant Latina women participating in the groups should be 18 years or older. Currently, there is no SYP curriculum for immigrant Latina teenagers. The scope of the manual is intended for young and adult immigrant Latina women over 18 years of age who speak Spanish. Legal status and self-identification as being in a DV relationship are not criteria for inclusion because this might deter participation.

Facilitators can decide whether they need administrative support for coordinating and recruiting participants for the psycho-educational group. Other administrative staff can help organize childcare, location of room, equipment needed, and weekly snack options for participants.

Assessment for domestic violence and safety planning

Facilitators should have a general knowledge base regarding DV assessment and intervention. The principle method used in DV assessment and intervention involves DV advocacy and empowerment (Pence, 2001; Walker, 1979, 2002).[9] The main components of DV advocacy and empowerment include (a) education (e.g., talking to participants about DV and having DV information available at the agency); (b) raising awareness on DV; (c) validating, supporting, and providing options to participants; and (d) safety planning and connecting participants with local resources in the community (e.g., mental health agencies or shelter information). Facilitators should educate participants on safety precautions (e.g., review safety plan handout) and remind participants of their option to call the local crisis center hotline or the local authorities if a situation becomes severe.

Although some participants may not be directly involved in relationships with DV incidences, it is important to assess for safety among all participants because of the high prevalence rates of DV among the Latino population. Therefore, an important component of the curriculum includes assessing for safety of the participants throughout the program and providing a weekly mental health/DV resource handout to participants who desire it.

Confidentiality and mandatory reporting

Facilitators should discuss with participants issues related to confidentiality. Facilitators must explain to participants the importance of keeping information that is shared among participants confidential. The motto often used is: "Whatever is said in the room stays in the room." Importantly, though, as licensed mental health professionals, we are required by state law to report to the local authorities any disclosure or suspicion related to childhood sexual abuse, sexual assault of a minor under the age of 18 years of age, childhood physical abuse and neglect, elder abuse and neglect, and suicidal or homicidal threats or gestures. We are mandated reporters, and participants should be aware of those incidences when we need to break confidentiality.

Mental health/domestic violence resource handout and information on legal issues

Group facilitators in social service agencies, community health clinics, faith-based programs, or other agencies should develop a mental health and DV resource handout for the facilitators to use in the psycho-educational group. The resource handout should include local crisis phone numbers, local shelter phone numbers, and the national phone number to the Domestic Violence Network (1-800-799-SAFE). The resource handout should include mental health agencies in the local community that provide individual counseling. Facilitators should also provide information on legal issues and immigrant Latina women's rights. Often, immigrant Latina women who lack legal status in the United States do not call local authorities because of fear of being deported, but they are misinformed about their rights. Facilitators should discuss these legal issues (e.g., the right to call the local police and/or file an order of protection with the police department is they feel unsafe or are threatened by an intimate partner). The resource handout should be given to participants at the initial intake meeting and throughout the weekly sessions. Appendix A illustrates a sample of a mental health/DV resource handout. Group facilitators should also create and provide a resource handout that includes local phone numbers in their respective communities and national DV phone numbers and websites that provide crisis intervention and shelter assistance. Appendix B includes phone numbers and websites facilitators can use on handouts.

Childcare and snacks for children and immigrant Latina women

The agency should provide childcare for the participants, as the participants and children benefit when childcare is provided. Women's inability to find high-quality, affordable childcare during the 11 weeks of the program is expected to be a principal deterrent to participation. The participants need time to think about themselves as women, assess their self-esteem, and discuss current relationships with other women. It is important that they take time for themselves free from the presence of their children. Findings from the research project examining immigrant Latina women's experiences with SYP curriculum indicate participants' satisfaction increased with the program when childcare and snacks were provided (Marrs Fuchsel, 2014a; Marrs Fuchsel & Hysjulien, 2013).[10]

Ongoing support after completion of program

Participants who complete the program might need additional ongoing therapeutic support and individual counseling. Facilitators should be familiar with community-based agencies that provide long-term individual counseling. Facilitators can support and assist participants who want information on individual counseling post completion of the program.

NOTES

1. Lieberman, M., & Golant, M. (2002). Leader behaviors as perceived by cancer patients in professionally directed support groups and outcomes. *Group Dynamics: Theory, Research, and Practice, 6,* 267–276. doi:10.1037//1089-2699.6.4.267; Robbins, R., Tonemah, S., & Robbins, S. (2002). Project eagle: Techniques for multi-family psycho-educational group. *American Indian and Alaska Native Mental Health Research, 10,* 56–74. doi:10.5820/aian.1003.2002.56; Toseland, R. W., & Rivas, R. F. (2017). *An introduction to group work practice: Connecting core competencies series* (8th ed.). Boston, MA: Pearson Education.

2. Robbins, R., Tonemah, S., & Robbins, S. (2002). Project eagle: Techniques for multi-family psycho-educational group. *American Indian and Alaska Native Mental Health Research, 10,* 56–74. doi:10.5820/aian.1003.2002.56; Toseland, R. W., & Rivas, R. F. (2017). *An introduction to group work practice: Connecting core competencies series* (8th ed.). Boston, MA: Pearson Education.

3. Toseland, R. W., & Rivas, R. F. (2017). *An introduction to group work practice: Connecting core competencies series* (8th ed.). Boston, MA: Pearson Education.

4. Kasturirangan, A. (2008). Empowerment and programs designed to address domestic violence. *Violence Against Women, 14,* 1465–1475. doi:10.1177/1077801208325188

5. Marrs Fuchsel, C. (2014a). "Yes, I have changed because I am more sure of myself, I feel stronger with more confidence and strength": Examining the experiences of immigrant Latina women participating in the *Sí, Yo Puedo* curriculum. *Journal of Ethnographic and Qualitative Research, 8,* 161–182; Marrs Fuchsel, C., & Hysjulien, B. (2013). Exploring a domestic violence intervention curriculum for immigrant Mexican women in a group setting: A pilot study. *Social Work with Groups, 36,* 304–320. doi 10.1080/01609513.2013.767130

6. Marrs Fuchsel, C., & Hysjulien, B. (2013). Exploring a domestic violence intervention curriculum for immigrant Mexican women in a group setting: A pilot study. *Social Work with Groups, 36,* 304–320. doi 10.1080/01609513.2013.767130

7. Marrs Fuchsel, C., & Hysjulien, B. (2013). Exploring a domestic violence intervention curriculum for immigrant Mexican women in a group setting: A pilot study. *Social Work with Groups, 36,* 304–320. doi 10.1080/01609513.2013.767130

8. Marrs Fuchsel, C., Linares, R., Abugattas, A., Padilla, M., & Hartenberg, L. (2015). *Sí, Yo Puedo* curricula: Latinas examining domestic violence and self. *Affilia: Journal of Women and Social Work, 31,* 219–231. doi:10.1177/0886109915608220

9. Pence, E. (2001). Advocacy on behalf of battered women. In C. M. Renzetti, J. L. Edleson, & R. K. Bergen (Eds.), *Sourcebook on violence against women* (pp. 329–343). Thousand Oaks, CA: SAGE; Walker, L. E. (2002). The politics of trauma practice: Politics, psychology and the battered woman's movement. *Journal of Trauma Practice, 1,* 81–102; Walker, L. E. (1979). *The battered woman.* New York: Harper & Row.

10. Marrs Fuchsel, C. (2014a). "Yes, I have changed because I am more sure of myself, I feel stronger with more confidence and strength": Examining the experiences of immigrant Latina women participating in the *Sí, Yo Puedo* curriculum. *Journal of Ethnographic and Qualitative Research, 8,* 161–182; Marrs Fuchsel, C., & Hysjulien, B. (2013). Exploring a domestic violence intervention curriculum for immigrant Mexican women in a group setting: A pilot study. *Social Work with Groups, 36,* 304–320. doi 10.1080/01609513.2013.767130

SÍ, YO PUEDO CURRICULUM, WEEKLY SESSIONS, INSTRUCTION, AND ACTIVITIES

5

PART I: AWARENESS OF SELF

Week 1: Introductions and Who Am I? Begin the discussion on identity and awareness of self. The participants develop group rules. Instruction: Teach values and beliefs. Self-reflection drawing or writing activity: Who am I?

Week 2: Coping Strategies. Begin the discussion on types of coping strategies. Instruction: Teach general definition of coping and teach positive and negative coping strategies (e.g., negative coping strategies such as alcohol or drugs). Teach the participants relaxation and deep breathing exercises. Self-reflection drawing or writing activity: Identify four problems and coping strategies.

Week 3: Self-esteem. Begin the discussion on what self-esteem is. Instruction: Teach general definition of self-esteem and assessment of current self-esteem. Self-reflection drawing or writing activity: What do you think and feel about yourself?

Week 4: Influences of Past Traumas. Begin the discussion of influences of past traumas on women's sense of self. For example, childhood sexual abuse or witnessing domestic violence (DV) in the home impact adult self-esteem, current relationships, and mental and physical health. Instruction: Teach on the dynamics and definition of sexual abuse, child abuse, or other types of traumas as identified by the participants. Self-reflection drawing or writing activity: Timeline activity.

PART II: KNOWLEDGE OF RELATIONSHIPS WITHIN CULTURE

Week 5: Dating. Begin the discussion on the dynamics of dating experiences within the Latino culture, parents' instruction regarding dating and influences such as parents, religion, or the media on dating experiences. Discuss participants' perspectives on dating and how they define dating. Instruction: Teach on characteristics of healthy dating and cite information from previous studies on Latinas' description of dating within the Latino community. Self-reflection drawing or writing activity: What does dating look like? What was your first dating experience like?

Week 6: Cultural Concepts: Familism, Machismo, and Marianismo. Begin the discussion on the cultural concepts of *familism, machismo,* and *marianismo* and how these may affect participants' knowledge of dating and healthy relationships. Instruction: Teach on what *familism, machismo,* and *marianismo* might look like in relationships and family life and cite information from previous studies on Latinas' description of the cultural influences on relationships. Self-reflection drawing or writing activity: Draw a picture or write about how cultural concepts influence women's understanding of relationships and dating. Alternate self-reflection drawing or writing activity: Genogram/identify family patterns.

Week 7: Healthy Relationships. Begin the discussion on what healthy relationships look like in dating and committed, romantic relationships. Instruction: Teach on characteristics of healthy relationships; use the Equality Wheel handout and healthy relationships characteristics handout. Self-reflection drawing or writing activity: Draw a picture of how you view your current relationship.

Week 8: Domestic Violence. Begin the discussion on what DV looks like. Instruction: Teach on the dynamics, definition, types of abuse found in DV and overall prevalence rates among immigrant Latina women experiencing DV (cite appropriately using statistical data). Discuss the importance of safety, safety planning, legal issues, and lethal situations. Use the Power and Control Wheel; give handouts on safety planning and mental health/DV services in the community. No self-reflection drawing or writing activity.

PART III: IMPACT OF FACTORS ON RELATIONSHIPS

Week 9: Factors Influencing Relationships. Begin the discussion on types of factors that influence women's understanding of relationships. Instruction: Teach on specific factors such as the media, parents, and religious institutions. Self-reflection drawing or writing activity: Factors influencing relationships; are they positive or negative influences?

Alternate topic: The facilitators should check in with the participants in the middle of the program to assess their interest in understanding the dynamics and definition of sexual abuse. If participants are interested in knowing more about sexual abuse and how to speak to their children on the prevention of sexual abuse, the facilitator should use the alternate topic of sexual abuse as opposed to the *Factors Influencing Relationships* session. Instruction: Teach definition of childhood sexual abuse, how to protect children (e.g., signs to look for), and how to access resources in the community. Address the challenges with reporting or not reporting incidences of childhood sexual abuse. No self-reflection drawing or writing exercises.

Week 10: Talking to Children. Begin the discussion on women's ability to talk to their children (girls and boys) about healthy dating. Instruction: Teach participants how to address sensitive topics with their children and how modeling healthy relationships is important in children's own understanding of what a healthy relationship looks like. Self-reflection drawing or writing activity: Draw a picture of a crystal ball and write a letter to your child. What will you say?

Week 11: Resources and Graduation. Begin the discussion on empowerment and changes that might have occurred since taking part in the program using the *Sí, Yo Puedo* (SYP) curriculum. Instruction: Review safety measures and mental health/DV resource handout. Self-reflection drawing or writing activity: Suitcase activity: What will you take with you? Participants receive a certificate of completion and a meal is provided. Participants share their experiences with the program; participants may exchange phone numbers, and group members process the experience as a group.

Use of Figures 5.1–5.49. Sample self-reflection drawing or writing activities followed by sample handouts are included in the weekly classes. Group facilitators are encouraged to use the sample self-reflection drawing or writing handouts with participants each week.

Additional suggested readings for group facilitators. For each of the weekly topics, group facilitators can review the suggested readings to help them with the specific content.

PART I: AWARENESS OF SELF

Week 1: Introductions and Who Am I?
Objectives.
1. Participants begin to understand who they are as women and the multiple roles they encompass. For example, women are mothers, girlfriends, wives, sisters, grandmothers, coworkers, and neighbors.
2. Participants begin the process of becoming a part of a group.
3. Participants learn about values and beliefs.

Group rules. The participants develop and create group rules. Example ground rules: Confidentiality ("everything that is said in the group stays in the group"); one person speaks at a time; everyone participates, listens, and is respectful; smart phones on vibrate.

Self-reflection drawing or writing activity. Who am I folder activity. Each class begins with a drawing or writing activity. In the first class, participants begin with the drawing or writing activity titled *Who Am I?* Participants discuss and share what their name represents. Participants are encouraged to write or draw their values and beliefs. Participants support and learn from one another as they share their folders. Participants can bring a picture of themselves or their family in Week 2. Participants can tape a picture on their folder and share the picture with group members.

Teaching and instruction. Teach values and beliefs and begin large-group discussion: What are values? What are beliefs? Write the responses on the board. For example, a value is "Family is important." A belief is "I believe in working hard and supporting my family back in my home country."

Create a review handout after each class. After class, write a summary of the comments and statements made by the participants in the group. The following week, give the participants the review handout that includes two to three reflection questions that they can do on their own in between classes.

Background information on identity, self-concept, and self-esteem. Information on *identity* is found in the social psychology literature that examines the social construct of *self-esteem* (i.e., how one person examines him/herself; Cast & Burke, 2002)[1] as part of the self-concept. There are two dimensions of self-esteem. The first is competence (i.e., the person examines his or her capacity to do something), and the second is worth (i.e., the person examines his or her value as a person and examines how he or she feels about him- or herself; Cast & Burke, 2002). In their article examining identity theory as a framework for examining concepts of self-esteem, Cast and Burke (2002) defined identity as "a set of meanings that represent the understandings, feelings, and expectations that are applied to the self as an occupant of a social position" (p. 1043).[2] It is important to understand self-concept and identity as part of self-esteem in the SYP curriculum because immigrant Latina women will benefit by understanding who they are as women and the multiple roles they identify with in their lives.

Additional suggested readings for group facilitators.

Counseling and family therapy with Latino populations: Strategies that work, by Robert Smith and R. Esteban Montilla. New York: Routledge, 2015.

Feminist therapy with Latina women: Personal and social voices, by Debra Kawahara and Oliva Espin. New York: Routledge, 2013.

Group work with populations at risk (3rd ed.), by Geoffrey Greif and Paul Ephross. New York: Oxford University Press, 2010.

Latino families in therapy (2nd ed.), by Celia Jaes Falicov. Guilford family therapy series. New York: Guilford Press, 2015.

No more secrets: A therapist's guide to group work with adult survivors of domestic violence, by Denise Grant and Irene Lebbad. Bloomington, IN: Balboa Press, 2015.

Week 1: Self-Reflection Drawing or Writing Activity: "Who Am I?" Folder

Goal. Participants learn about values and beliefs, and they discuss topics related to identity and awareness of self, using the "Who Am I" folder activity.

Instructions. Participants draw or write about their name on a manila file folder. What does their name represent? Who named them? Participants draw or write important parts of their name. For example, women might consider the cultural importance or the religious importance of their name. Activity time: 10–15 minutes. (See Figures 5.1–5.4).

Materials needed for activity. File folders (manila), markers, pens, tape, scissors, and stickers.

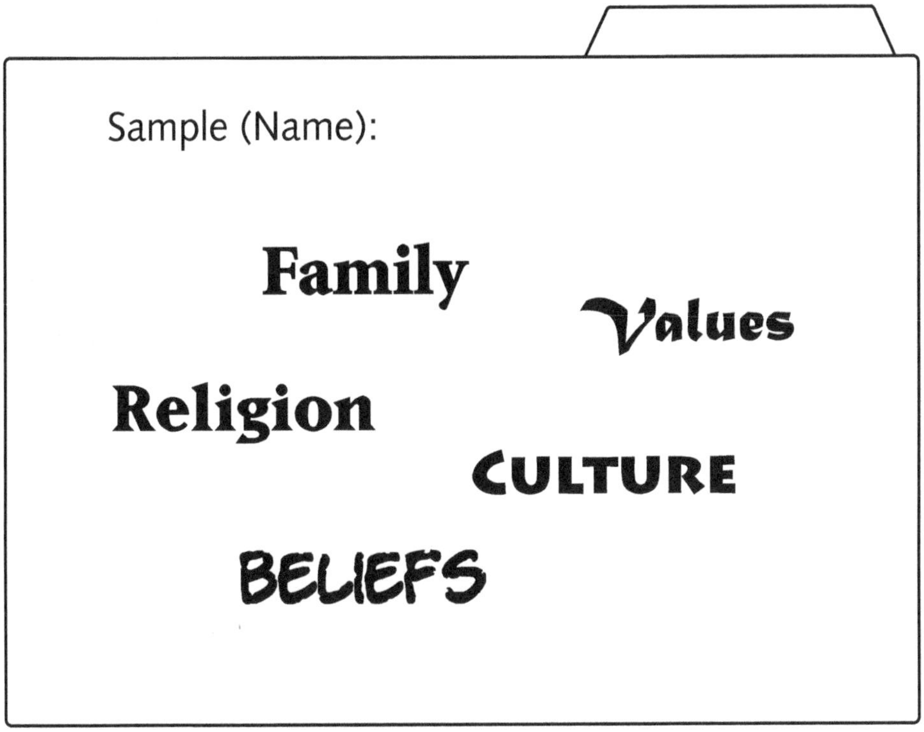

Sample (Name):

Family

Values

Religion

CULTURE

BELIEFS

FIGURE 5.1   Week 1: Sample Self-Reflection Drawing or Writing Activity
"Who am I?" folder

Name:

FIGURE 5.2   Week 1: Sample Self-Reflection Drawing or Writing Handout
"Who am I?" folder

Ejemplo (Nombre):

Familia

Valores

Religión

CULTURA

CREENCIAS

FIGURE 5.3 Semana 1: Ejemplo de auto reflexión—Ilustrar o detallar una actividad

Carpeta: ¿Quién soy yo?

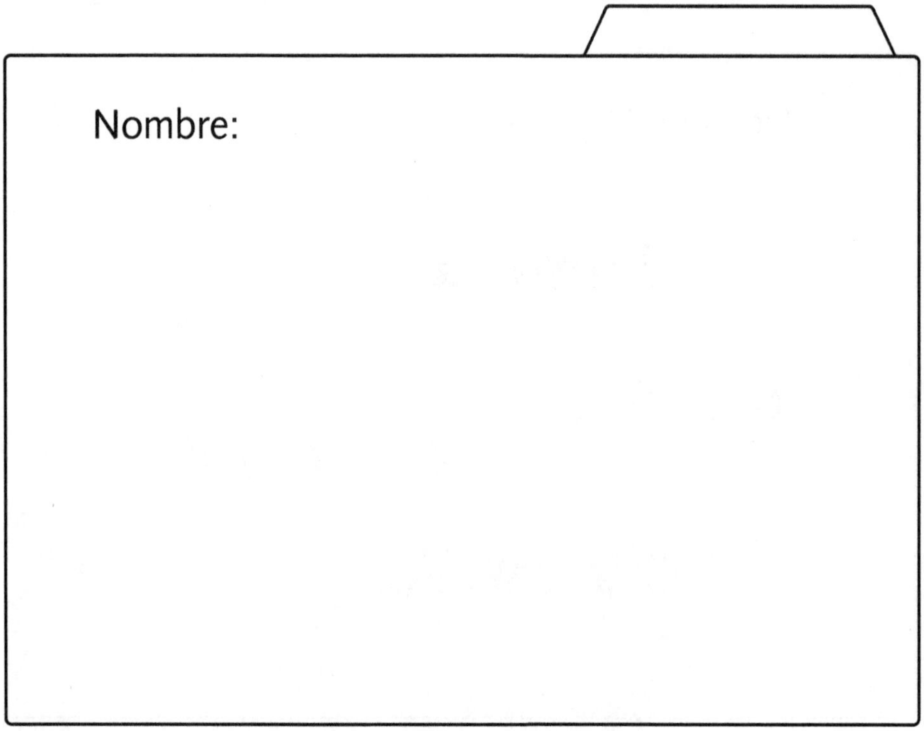

Nombre:

FIGURE 5.4 Semana 1: Ejemplo de auto reflexión—Ilustrar o escribir en el folleto
Carpeta: ¿Quién soy yo?

Week 1: Sample Review Handout

Week 1: Introductions and Who Am I?

Values in group. Cultural values, religious values, mother's influence on values, responsible, hard worker, faithful, honest, trustworthy, material values.

Beliefs in group. I believe in family. I believe in helping my family in my home country. I believe in my children and supporting them as best as I can.

THINKING EXERCISES

1. I believe in (my beliefs):

_____

_____

_____

_____

_____

2. My values are:

_____

_____

_____

_____

_____

Week 2: Coping Strategies

Review handout. Pass out review handout from Week 1. Discuss with participants briefly the topic area from the previous week. Encourage participants to do the thinking exercises in between classes.

Objectives.

1. Participants begin to understand coping strategies and how to manage problems.
2. Participants understand negative and positive coping skills.
3. Participants understand stress.
4. Participants learn relaxation and breathing techniques.

Self-reflection drawing or writing activity. Participants draw or write about four problems and articulate how they manage the problems. Participants are asked to identify positive or negative ways of coping. An alternate drawing activity is the eco-map. Eco-maps are used to assess relationships and the physical environment. Participants identify problem areas as they reflect on relationships and areas of their life. Participants share their drawing or writing activity and learn from one another.

Teaching and instruction. Teach and discuss positive and negative coping skills and how to manage problems. Teach and discuss stress and the impact of stress on work, family, and mental and physical health. Teach deep breathing exercises. Write the responses on the board or flipchart. For example, a positive coping skill is talking with someone about problems. A negative coping skill is drinking too much after work.

Create a review handout after each class. After class, write a summary of the comments and statements made by the participants in the group. The following week, give the participants the review handout that includes two to three reflection questions that they can do on their own in between classes.

Background information on coping strategies. The use of coping mechanisms is important in managing stress, social roles among women, and symptoms of disorders such as depression (Aranda, Castaneda, Lee, & Sobel, 2001).[3] A review of the literature indicates that individuals experience two types of coping mechanisms: (a) approach coping (i.e., identifying the stressor and using strategies such as social support and seeking out medical attention) and (b) avoidance coping (i.e., escape coping such as not talking about a problem or drinking too much; Aranda et al., 2001). Individuals using approach coping to manage stressors and depressive symptoms tend to have fewer emotional and behavioral problems, whereas individuals using avoidance coping experience more psychological distress (Aranda et al., 2001).[4] Immigrant Latina women experience stressors and symptoms of disorders in relationships and in their social roles. Examining coping strategies is useful in helping immigrant Latina women understand the importance of effective coping strategies. An important consideration is the social support of spirituality and faith-based institutions in managing stressors. Immigrant Latina women likely use formal support systems such as priests or pastors in the Catholic Church or other Christian churches to help them manage stressors (Marrs Fuchsel, 2012).[5]

Additional suggested readings for group facilitators.

Mindfulness-oriented interventions for trauma: Integrating contemplative practices, by Victoria Follette, John Briere, Deborah Rozelle, James Hopper, and David Rome. New York: Guilford Press, 2014.

The relaxation and stress reduction workbook, by Martha Davis and Elizabeth Robbins Eshelman. Oakland, CA: New Harbinger, 2008.

Week 2: Self-Reflection Drawing or Writing Activity: Identify Problems/How Do I Cope?

Goal. Participants learn about problems impacting their life and identify positive and negative coping skills.

Instructions. Participants identify four problems (e.g., work stress, relationship problems, raising children). Participants identify what they do to manage problems. Participants identify positive or negative skills. Participants draw or write words. Write the answers on a board.

Alternative drawing activity. Facilitators can do an eco-map, a visual representation of an individual's interaction with the environment, structural systems, groups, and other persons (e.g., family member, social groups, community organizations, physical location, and work; Forte, 2007)[6] with participants to asses and identify problem areas that may cause stress. Activity time: 10–15 minutes. (See Figures 5.5–5.12).

Sample

Identify 4 problems

Identify positive and negative coping skills

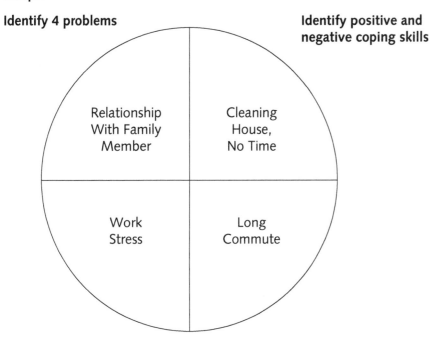

Relationship With Family Member

Cleaning House, No Time

Work Stress

Long Commute

FIGURE 5.5 Week 2: Sample Self-Reflection Drawing or Writing Activity
Identify problems/How do you cope?

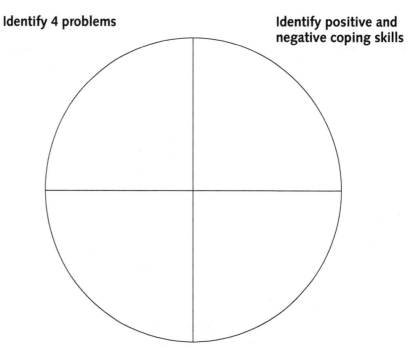

Identify 4 problems

Identify positive and negative coping skills

FIGURE 5.6 Week 2: Sample Self-Reflection Drawing or Writing Handout Identify problems/How do you cope?

YES, I CAN (*SÍ, YO PUEDO*)

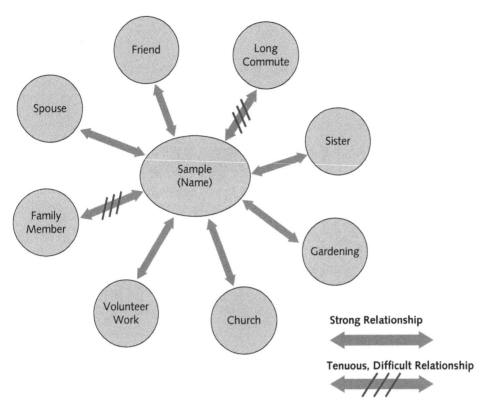

FIGURE 5.7 Week 2: Sample Self-Reflection Alternative Drawing or Writing Activity

Eco-map to assess person in the environment and identify problem areas

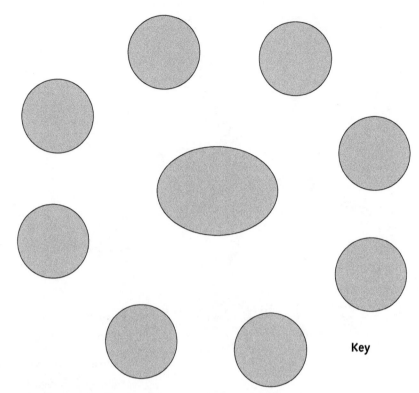

Key

FIGURE 5.8   Week 2: Sample Self-Reflection Alternative Drawing or Writing Handout
Eco-map to assess the physical environment and identify problem areas

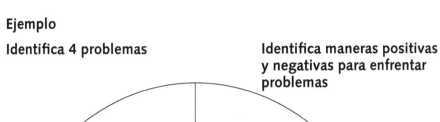

Ejemplo

Identifica 4 problemas

Identifica maneras positivas y negativas para enfrentar problemas

Relación con los miembros de la familia

Limpiar la casa, no hay tiempo

Estres por el trabajo

Recorridos largos

FIGURE 5.9 Semana 2: Ejemplo de auto reflexión—Ilustrar o detallar una actividad
Identificar problemas ¿Cómo puedo manejar los problemas?

Identifica 4 problemas

Identifica maneras positivas y negativas para enfrentar problemas

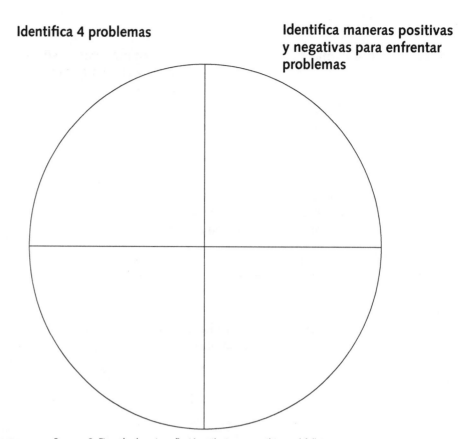

FIGURE 5.10 Semana 2: Ejemplo de auto reflexión—Ilustrar o escribir en el folleto Identifica problemas ¿Cómo puedo manejar los problemas?

YES, I CAN (*SÍ, YO PUEDO*)

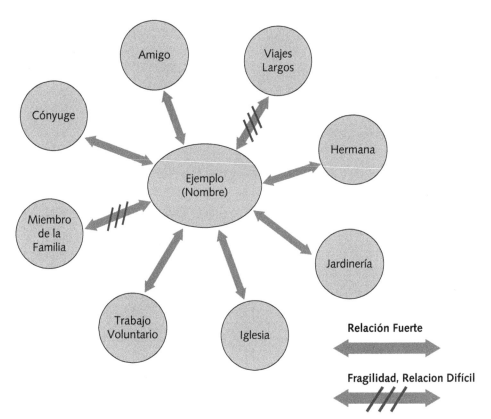

Relación Fuerte

Fragilidad, Relacion Difícil

FIGURE 5.11   Semana 2: Ejemplo de auto reflexión—Alternativa, Ilustrar o detallar una actividad

Eco-mapa para evaluar a la persona en su ambiente e identificar sus problemas

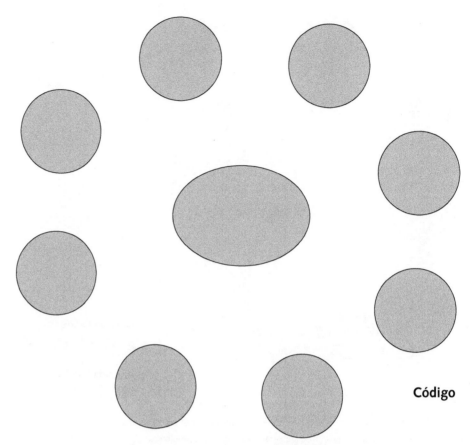

Código

FIGURE 5.12   Semana 2: Ejemplo de auto reflexión—Alternativa, Ilustrar o escribir en el folleto
Eco-mapa para evaluar a la persona en su ambiente e identificar sus problemas

Week 2: Sample Review Handout

Empowerment Group; Date_____

Week 2: Coping Strategies

How to manage problems. Talk to a friend, prayer, faith, listen, cry, be positive, feel, experience feelings, know that it is a process, seek help, talk to someone, receive support, exercise, relax.

Types of problems identified. For example, problems in relationships with children, spouse/partner, or other family members. Other types of problems include finances, health, weight, inability to obtain work, lack of educational attainment, immigration-related issues, moving, and divorce and past experiences that might influence present adult behavior.

THINKING EXERCISES

1. How do I manage my problems? Are some negative coping skills? How do I make them positive skills?

_____

_____

_____

_____

_____

Week 3: Self-Esteem

Review handout. Pass out review handout from Week 2. Discuss with participants briefly the topic area from the previous week. Encourage participants to do the thinking exercises in between classes.

Objectives.
1. Participants understand self-esteem
2. Participants identify characteristics of self-esteem.
3. Participants understand feelings.
4. Participants experience awareness of self and how they feel about themselves.

Self-reflection drawing or writing activity. Participants draw a picture of themselves. Participants draw or write three parts of self-esteem. First, participants write what they like about themselves and what they like to do. Second, participants write what people like about them and what they do well. Third, participants write what they do well. Participants share their drawing or writing activity and learn from one another. Instruct the participants to bring their favorite picture of themselves the following week. Participants will tape the picture on the drawing activity, and they will share the picture with group members.

Teaching and instruction. Teach and discuss the definition of self-esteem. Discuss with participants factors that contribute to self-esteem (e.g., parenting in childhood, attachment patterns, and traumatic experiences such as physical childhood abuse or sexual abuse). Discuss with participants how they currently feel about themselves. Write the responses on the board. For example, "Self-esteem is how I think and feel about myself."

Create a review handout after each class. After class, write a summary of the comments and statements made by the participants in the group. The following week, give the participants the review handout that includes two to three reflection questions that they can do on their own in between classes.

Background information on self-esteem. (See background information in Week 1).

Additional suggested readings for group facilitators.

50 mindful steps to self-esteem: Everyday practices for cultivating self-acceptance and self-compassion, by Janetti Marotta. Oakland, CA: New Harbinger, 2013.

Week 3: Self-Reflection Drawing or Writing Activity:
What Do I Think and Feel about Myself?

Goal. Participants learn about self-esteem. Participants reflect on how they view themselves, and they discuss their understanding of self-esteem with peers.

Instructions. Participants draw a picture of themselves and answer three questions: (a) What do I like about myself? (b) What do people like about me and what do they say that I do well? and (c) What can I do really well? Participants draw or write words. Activity time: 10–15 minutes. (See Figures 5.13–5.16).

FIGURE 5.13 Week 3: Sample Self-Reflection Drawing or Writing Activity

What do I think and feel about myself?

YES, I CAN (*SÍ, YO PUEDO*)

FIGURE 5.14 Week 3: Sample Self-Reflection Drawing or Writing Handout
What do I think and feel about myself?

FIGURE 5.15 Semana 3: Ejemplo de auto reflexión—Ilustrar o detallar una actividad

¿Qué es lo que pienso y siento acerca de mí misma?

YES, I CAN (*SÍ, YO PUEDO*)

FIGURE 5.16   Semana 3: Ejemplo de auto reflexión—Ilustrar o escribir en el folleto

¿Qué es lo que pienso y siento acerca de mí misma?

Empowerment Group; Date_____

Week 3: Self-Esteem

Defining self-esteem: How you feel or think about yourself.

Strategies to increase self-esteem: Positive self-talk, write, draw, exercise, belief in self, obtain sunshine, taking time to care for mental and physical health, participating in hobbies, accepting and loving self, ignoring negativity from others, and being around positive people. Seek out professional help.

THINKING EXERCISES

1. What do I like about myself?

_____

_____

_____

_____

_____

2. What do other people say about me?

_____

_____

_____

_____

_____

Week 4: Influences of Past Trauma

Review handout. Pass out review handout from Week 3. Discuss with participants briefly the topic area from the previous week. Encourage participants to do the thinking exercises in between classes.

Note: Participants tape the picture on the drawing activity from the previous week (self-esteem). Participants share the picture with each other.

Objectives.

1. Participants understand how past childhood traumas influence adult present behavior, thoughts, feelings, and attitudes.
2. Participants identify types of past traumas such as experiencing sexual abuse, witnessing DV, poverty, divorce, serious mental or physical illness of a parent, and emotional neglect.
3. Participants experience awareness of past traumas on their present identity and sense of self.

Self-reflection drawing or writing activity. Participants draw a timeline of experiences from infancy to their present age in decade-long increments. Participants write or draw experiences between the ages of infancy to 10 years of age; 10–20 years of age; 20–30 years of age; 30–40 years of age; 40–50 years of age; 50–60 years of age; and 60 and older. Participants reflect on experiences that were difficult and challenging and that might have endangered their sense of safety as children and adolescents. Participants share their drawing or writing activity and learn from one another.

Teaching and instruction. Teach on the definition of *trauma* (i.e., an emotional or psychological injury, usually resulting from an extremely stressful or life-threatening situation). Trauma in childhood (e.g., childhood sexual abuse) often affects normal development in childhood and adolescence. Discuss the characteristics of traumatic experiences and the impact of challenging experiences on present mental and physical well-being. Teach on the definition of *resilience* (i.e., the ability to recover from adversity and difficult life experiences). Each person experiences resiliency in different ways. Discuss the probability of experiencing emotional distress in this class. Use grounding skills and breathing exercises to manage difficult emotions in class. Write the responses on the board or flipchart.

Create a review handout after each class. After class, write a summary of the comments and statements made by the participants in the group. The following week, give the participants the review handout that includes two to three reflection questions that they can do on their own in between classes.

Background information on trauma and mental health. A review of the literature indicates a correlation between incidences of DV and symptoms of mental health disorders (Figley, 2012; Gorde, Helfrich & Finlayson, 2004; Humphreys & Thiara, 2003).[7] Depression, anxiety, substance abuse, posttraumatic stress disorder, and other mental health disorders (i.e., personality disorders, somatization, and obsessive-compulsive disorders) are commonly found among victims of DV (Figley, 2013; Gorde, et al., 2004).[8] In addition, a DV incident can be a traumatic experience (e.g., a physical or sexual assault in a relationship; Figley, 2013). An understanding of the correlation between DV and symptoms of mental health disorders is important because of the implications on current relationships and on immigrant Latina women's ability to seek out mental health services. In addition, the examination of influences of past trauma among immigrant Latina women will help them gain a deeper understanding of how past traumas might influence current relationships and self-esteem.

Additional suggested readings for group facilitators.

Counseling and family therapy with Latino populations: Strategies that work, by Robert Smith and R. Esteban Montilla. New York: Routledge, 2015.

Invisible violence: Special issues in intimate partner violence among Latino families living in the U.S., by Joanna Morse. Saarbrücken, Germany: Lambert Academic, 2009.

Mindfulness-oriented interventions for trauma: Integrating contemplative practices, by Victoria Follette, John Briere, Deborah Rozelle, James Hopper, and David Rome. New York: Guilford Press, 2014.

No more secrets: A therapist's guide to group work with adult survivors of domestic violence, by Denise Grant and Irene Lebbad. Bloomington, IN: Balboa Press, 2015.

Week 4: Self-Reflection Drawing or Writing Activity: Timeline

Goal. Participants identify and reflect on influences of past traumas and if they experienced difficult life experiences.

Instructions. Participants draw a line with specific ages. Participants identify challenging experiences throughout their life. The following question is asked to begin the reflection process: Did anything happen to you that was very difficult during those times? Participants draw or write words. Activity time: 10–15 minutes. (See Figures 5.17–5.20).

Sample: Name

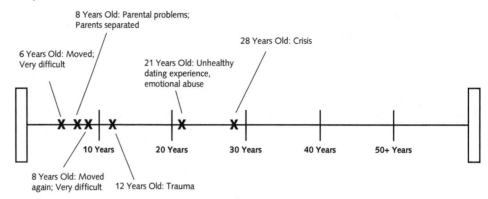

FIGURE 5.17 Week 4: Sample Self-Reflection Drawing or Writing Activity Timeline: Think about difficult experiences from the past

FIGURE 5.18 Week 4: Sample Self-Reflection Drawing or Writing Handout Timeline: Think about difficult experiences from the past

YES, I CAN (*SÍ, YO PUEDO*)

Ejemplo: Nombre

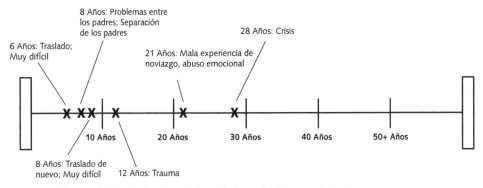

FIGURE 5.19   Semana 4: Ejemplo de auto reflexión—Ilustrar o detallar una actividad

Línea de tiempo: Pensar en experiencias difíciles del pasado

FIGURE 5.20   Semana 4: Ejemplo de auto reflexión—Ilustrar o escribir en el folleto

Línea de tiempo: Pensar en experiencias difíciles del pasado

Empowerment Group; Date_____

Week 4: Influences of Past Traumas

Types of traumatic experiences. Sexual abuse, witnessing DV, verbal and emotional abuse, physical abuse, childhood abuse, divorce, death, other types of violence, abandonment of children by parental figure, poverty, illness (e.g., physical and mental illness), neglect, moving to another country.

Overcoming traumatic experiences. Seeking professional help, support from friends and family members, journaling, talking with a trusted person, acknowledging difficult experiences of the past, accepting a difficult experience, learning about recovery, prayer, faith, exercise, and proper nutrition.

THINKING EXERCISES

1. What are some of my traumas?

_____

_____

_____

_____

_____

2. What has helped me overcome and manage childhood trauma?

_____

_____

_____

_____

_____

PART II: KNOWLEDGE OF RELATIONSHIPS WITHIN CULTURE

Week 5: Dating

Review handout. Pass out review handout from Week 4. Discuss with participants briefly the topic area from the previous week. Encourage participants to do the thinking exercises in between classes.

Objectives.
1. Participants understand what dating looks like within their own culture.
2. Participants identify characteristics of dating experiences from their lived experience.
3. Participants understand parental influence on dating experiences.
4. Participants discuss and reflect on external factors that influence dating experiences (e.g., religion, media, societal rules and norms, extended family members).

Self-reflection drawing or writing activity. Participants draw or write about their first dating experience or what dating looks like within their own culture. Participants draw a picture of themselves and reflect on a dating experience. Participants describe positive or negative characteristics of dating experiences. Participants share their drawing or writing activity and learn from one another.

Teaching and instruction. Teach on characteristics of healthy teen dating using Appendix C, the Equality Wheel for Teens and Teen Power and Control Wheel (National Center on Domestic and Sexual Violence, 2013).[9] Teach and discuss positive and negative characteristics of dating. Discuss and review safety issues in dating experiences. Write the responses on the board. For example, a positive characteristic of a healthy dating experience might include *mutual respect*.

Create a review handout after each class. After class, write a summary of the comments and statements made by the participants in the group. The following week, give the participants the review handout that includes two to three reflection questions that they can do on their own in between classes.

Background information on dating with a cultural perspective. Umaña-Taylor and Fine's (2003)[10] review of the literature indicated that most Latino couples are committed to marrying their first dating partner; thus they have an opportunity to discuss the dating phenomena with parents before committing to marriage—this discussion may be useful for immigrant Latina women in understanding healthy romantic relationships. Limited information is available regarding immigrant Latina women's experiences with the phenomenon of dating, reasons for entering into marriage, and parental influence on commitment to marriage; however, one study examined the relations among acculturation, gender stereotypes, and attitudes about dating violence in dating among urban Latina/o youth (Ulloa, Jaycox, Skinner, & Orsburn, 2008).[11] Ulloa et al.'s (2008) findings indicated that boys were more accepting of dating violence, whereas females reported more belief in gender egalitarianism. It is important to examine immigrant Latina women's experiences with the dating phenomenon within a cultural framework because of the implications on future healthy relationships.

Additional suggested readings for group facilitators.

Boundaries in dating: How healthy choices grow healthy relationships, by Henry Cloud and John Townsend. Grand Rapids, MI: Zondervan, 2000.

Group work with populations at risk (3rd ed.), by Geoffrey Greif and Paul Ephross. New York: Oxford University Press, 2010.

National Latin@ Network website. http://www.nationallatinonetwork.org/

Week 5: Self-Reflection Drawing or Writing Activity: Dating

What does dating look like? Or write about your first dating experience.

Goal. Participants identify and reflect on dating experience, in particular, their first dating experience.

Instructions. Participants draw a picture of what dating looks like. The following prompts are given to begin the reflection process: (a) Describe your first dating experience. (b) What did your mother or father tell you about dating? Activity time: 10–15 minutes. (See Figures 5.21–5.24).

Sample: (Name)

What was my first experience with dating?
What did I want it to look like?

Was it Positive? Negative?

Happy

I was attracted
to the person.

Hormones

I liked the person.

Can't stop thinking
about it.

FIGURE 5.21 Week 5: Sample Self-Reflection Drawing or Writing Activity
What does dating look like? Or write about your first dating experience.

**What was my first experience with dating?
What did I want it to look like?**

Was it Positive? Negative?

FIGURE 5.22 Week 5: Sample Self-Reflection Drawing or Writing Handout
What does dating look like? Or write about your first dating experience.

Ejemplo (Nombre)

¿Cuál fue mi experiencia en mi primera cita?
¿Cómo me hubiera gustado que fuera?

¿Fue positiva?
¿O Negativa?

Feliz

Hormonas

Me sentí atraída
por la persona.

Me gustó la persona.

No puedo dejar
de pensar en ello.

FIGURE 5.23   Semana 5: Ejemplo de auto reflexión—Ilustrar o detallar una actividad

¿Cómo veo las citas de enamoramiento? Escribe sobre la experiencia de tu primera cita.

¿Cuál fue mi experiencia en mi primera cita?
¿Cómo me hubiera gustado que fuera?

¿Fue positiva?
¿O Negativa?

FIGURE 5.24   Semana 5: Ejemplo de auto reflexión—Ilustrar o escribir en el folleto

¿Cómo veo las citas de enamoramiento? Escribe sobre la experiencia de tu primera cita.

Week 5: Dating

First dating experience. Feelings of happiness, joy, letter writing, phone calls, courtship behavior.

Positive and negative dating experiences. Positive experiences include mutual respect, openness, communication, interest, and attraction. Negative dating experiences include verbal abuse, physical and sexual abuse.

Influences of dating experiences. Mothers, fathers, society, and media influence dating experiences. *Machismo* influences dating in the Latino community.

THINKING EXERCISES

1. How was my first dating experience?

_____

_____

_____

_____

_____

2. If it was not positive, how should it have gone?

_____

_____

_____

_____

_____

Week 6: Cultural Concepts: *Familism, Machismo,* and *Marianismo*

Review handout. Pass out review handout from Week 5. Discuss with participants briefly the topic area from the previous week. Encourage participants to do the thinking exercises in between classes.

Objectives.

1. Participants identify and discuss cultural concepts such as familism, machismo, and marianismo.
2. Participants understand and reflect on how *familism, machismo,* and *marianismo* might impact relationships and dating experiences.
3. Participants reflect on characteristics of *familism, machismo,* and *marianismo.*

Self-reflection drawing or writing activity. Participants draw or write experiences with *familism, machismo,* and *marianismo.* An alternate drawing is a Genogram, a representation of an individual's family relationships in order to examine patterns of behavior (hereditary and psychological traits) among family members (McGoldrick, Gerson, & Petry, 2008).[12] The Genogram might help participants identify familial patterns of *familism, machismo,* and *marianismo* among family members. Participants share their drawing or writing activity and learn from one another.

Teaching and instruction. Discuss cultural concepts of *familism, machismo,* and *marianismo* and the impact on relationship dynamics and dating experiences. Write the responses on the board. For example, a *machismo* characteristic might include a behavior of dominance or superiority.

Create a review handout after each class. After class, write a summary of the comments and statements made by the participants in the group. The following week, give the participants the review handout that includes two to three reflection questions that they can do on their own in between classes.

Background information on *familism* and *machismo*. Several authors reported on the concept of *familism* as an important cultural aspect in the experiences of immigrant Mexican women and DV (Brabeck & Guzmán, 2009; Klevens et al., 2007; Vidales, 2010).[13] Brabeck and Guzmán (2009)[14] examined women's help-seeking behaviors within a sociocultural context and concluded that participants with higher levels of *familism* sought out informal help more frequently than those with lower levels. The social construct of *familism* is a source of strength for many immigrant Latina women; however, this phenomenon of *familism* needs further investigation with regard to whether having a tight-knit family and an extended supportive family network assists or exacerbates potential acts of DV while women are pursuing a partner. Marrs Fuchsel et al. (2012)[15] found that immigrant Mexican women attempted to reach out for help to informal support systems (i.e., the family) but felt embarrassed to do so and did not access assistance from the family.

Vidales (2010)[16] examined the multiple challenges faced by immigrant Latinas experiencing DV and addressed how cultural beliefs such as *machismo* and *marianismo* and traditional gender roles affected their perceptions of DV and help-seeking behaviors. Results showed that women were more accepting of traditional gender roles. For example, one participant believed in the idea that husbands were entitled to physically harm their wives. In another study,

Kulkarni (2007)[17] examined the lives of young adolescent mothers and their experiences with parenting and commitment to remain with current partners despite emotional and physical DV incidences. Among Latina adolescents, specific cultural factors such as *marianismo* influenced their understanding to remain in relationships despite DV incidences. Examining these cultural concepts with parents and families and how they contribute to men's and women's behavior in relationships is important for immigrant Latina women. Immigrant Latina women may be able to detect these characteristics and may stop a DV experience.

Additional suggested readings for group facilitators.

Counseling and family therapy with Latino populations: Strategies that work, by Robert Smith and R. Esteban Montilla. New York: Routledge 2015.

Grief therapy with Latinos: Integrating culture for clinicians, by Carmen Iona Vazquez and Dinelia Rosa. New York: Springer, 2011.

Healing from violence: Latino men's journey to a new masculinity, by Christauria Welland and Neil Ribner. New York: Springer, 2007.

Sin golpes: Cómo transformer la respuesta violenta de los hombres en la pareja y la familia, by C. Welland and D. Wexler. Ciudad de México: Editorial Pax Mexico, 2007.

Week 6: Self-Reflection Drawing or Writing Activity: Cultural Concepts

Draw a picture or write about how cultural concepts influence women's understanding of relationships and dating.

Goal. Participants will begin to understand how *familism, machismo,* and *marianismo* might influence relationships and dating experiences. Participants will gain awareness and education around cultural concepts.

Instructions: Participants will draw a picture of themselves and write or draw how *familism, machismo,* and *marianismo* influence their understanding of relationships and dating experiences. Participants answer the following questions: (a) What are some negative or positive characteristics of *machismo* and/or *marianismo*? (b) Do these traits help me or not? (c) What does the culture say about *machismo* and/or *marianismo*? (d) Does my family help me or not in my relationship? (e) What does my family say? Activity time: 10–15 minutes. (See Figures 5.25–5.32).

FIGURE 5.25 Week 6: Sample Self-Reflection Drawing or Writing Activity

Draw a picture or write how cultural concepts influence women's understanding of relationships and dating

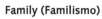

Family (Familismo)

Machismo

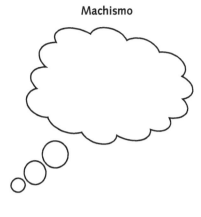

Marianismo

FIGURE 5.26 Week 6: Sample Self-Reflection Drawing or Writing Handout

Draw a picture or write how cultural concepts influence women's understanding of relationships and dating

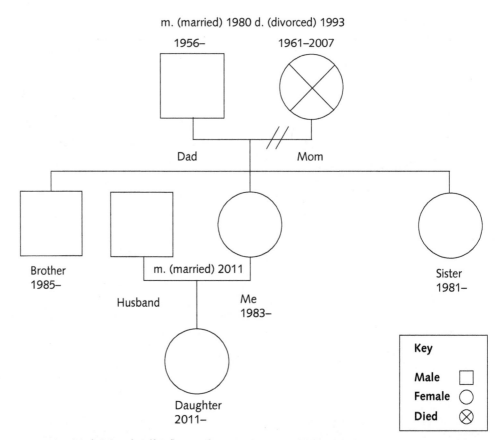

FIGURE 5.27 Week 6: Sample Self-Reflection Alternative Drawing or Writing Activity Genogram: Identify family patterns

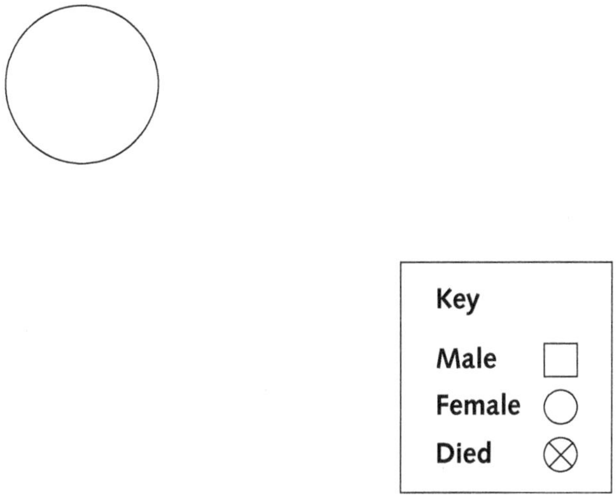

┌─────────────────────┐
│ **Key**   │
│   │
│ **Male**   ☐   │
│ **Female** ◯   │
│ **Died**   ⊗   │
└─────────────────────┘

FIGURE 5.28 Week 6: Sample Self-Reflection Alternative Drawing or Writing Handout
Genogram: Identify family patterns

Familia (Familismo)

¿Me ayudan o no en mi relación?
¿Qué es lo que ellos dicen?

Machismo

¿Negativo? ¿Positivo?
¿Me ayuda o no?
¿Qué es lo que la cultura dice?

Marianismo

¿Me ayuda o no?
¿Qué es lo que la cultura dice al respecto?

Ejemplo (Nombre)

FIGURE 5.29 Semana 6: Ejemplo de auto reflexión—Ilustrar o detallar una actividad

Escribe o dibuja cómo los conceptos culturales influyen en la comprensión de las mujeres sobre las relaciones y el enamoramiento

Familia (Familismo)

Machismo

Marianismo

FIGURE 5.30 Semana 6: Ejemplo de auto reflexión—Ilustrar o escribir en el folleto

Escribe o dibuja cómo los conceptos culturales influyen en la comprensión de las mujeres sobre las relaciones y el enamoramiento

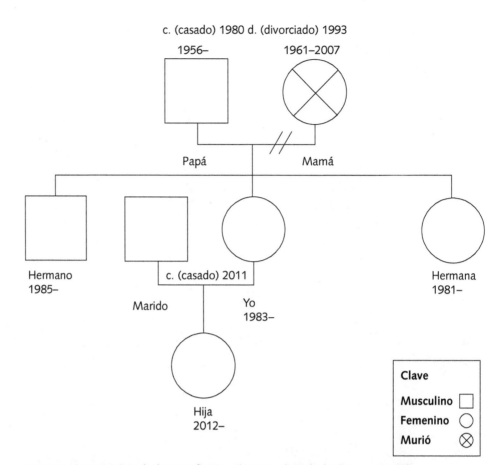

FIGURE 5.31 Semana 6: Ejemplo de auto reflexión—Alternativa, Ilustrar o detallar una actividad

Genograma: Identificar los patrones familiares

Clave

Musculino ☐

Femenino ○

Murió ⊗

FIGURE 5.32 Semana 6: Ejemplo de auto reflexión—Alternativa, Ilustrar o escribir en el folleto
Genograma: Identificar los patrones familiares

Empowerment Group; Date_____

Week 6: Cultural Concepts of *Familism, Machismo,* and *Marianimso*

Positive and negative characteristics of *machismo* and *marianismo*. Supportive, protective of wife, family, and children. Financial responsibility to the family, respectful, loves wife and children. Examples of negative characteristics of *machismo* include controlling behavior, manipulation, cultural, or being "macho." One positive characteristic of *marianismo* includes mothers being protective of their family and children. One negative characteristic of *marianismo* might be that women experience feeling submissive.

Positive and negative characteristics of *familism*. Positive characteristics include receiving support from extended family members. Difficulty disclosing DV-related incidences or childhood sexual abuse because of not disrupting family harmony in the larger family system.

Book recommendation in class. *The Female Brain,* by Louann Brizendine (Redondo Beach, CA: Morgan Road Books, 2007). Provides a biological understanding of the different behaviors between men and women.

THINKING EXERCISES

1. What has been my experience with *machismo* and/or *marianismo*?

_____

_____

_____

_____

_____

2. What has been my experience with *familism*?

_____

_____

_____

_____

_____

Week 7: Healthy Relationships

Review handout. Pass out review handout from Week 6. Discuss with participants briefly the topic area from the previous week. Encourage participants to do the thinking exercises in between classes.

Objectives.
1. Participants examine current relationships.
2. Participants gain awareness on characteristics of healthy relationships.
3. Participants discuss positive and negative characteristics of relationships.
4. Review Characteristics of Healthy Relationships handout. The Appendix D handout depits characteristics of healthy relationships (Arizona Coalition Against Domestic Violence, 2002).[18]

Self-reflection drawing or writing activity. Participants draw a picture of how they view their current relationship.

Teaching and instruction. Discuss characteristics of healthy relationships. Use the Characteristics of Healthy Relationship handout. Discuss with participants the term *love* and what it looks like. Write the responses on the board. For example, mutual respect is a characteristic of a healthy romantic relationship.

Create a review handout after each class. After class, write a summary of the comments and statements made by the participants in the group. The following week, give the participants the review handout that includes two to three reflection questions that they can do on their own in between classes.

Background information on healthy relationships. A review of the literature on healthy relationships has examined key concepts such as healthy relationships, couples, families, and marriage (Antle, Karam, Christensen, Barbee, & Bibhuti, 2011; Beck & Clark, 2010; Young, 2004).[19] For example, Young (2004)[20] reviewed research articles identifying characteristics of healthy relationships. Findings indicated that effective communication, awareness, intimacy, mutual trust between partners, and a sense of total security between partners were important characteristics in the healthfulness of relationships (Young, 2004).[21] Bagarozzi (1997) stated,

> Therefore, if true intimacy is to be part of a healthy couple relationship, each partner must feel totally secure in sharing his or her innermost thoughts, feelings, and self-disclosures with his or her partner without the fear of being judged, evaluated, or ridiculed. In addition to knowing that one's partner is open and receptive to whatever is shared, one must also feel that one's partner is reciprocating on similar levels of self-disclosure for intimacy to be maintained. (as cited in Young, 2004, p. 160)[22]

Another important characteristic of a healthy relationship is the ability to compare and contrast similarities and differences within each other and have dialogue about the differences, as opposed to viewing those differences as good or bad characteristics (Young, 2004).[23] Finally, Shumway and Wampler (2002) explained that it is both the behavior and how each partner experiences the behavior that determines a healthy relationship. These authors posited six important theoretical constructs in relationship satisfaction, including, "greeting and calling the partner by name, talking to the partner about common events, praising the partner, sharing memories, doing things together, and providing appropriate feedback" (as cited in

Young, 2004, p. 160).[24] By understanding characteristics of healthy relationships, immigrant Latina women will have a better understanding of the importance of examining current relationships and what they look like.

Additional suggested readings for group facilitators.

Counseling and family therapy with Latino populations:Strategies that work, by Robert Smith and R. Esteban Montilla. New York: Routledge, 2015.

Latina power: Using your 7 strengths to say no to abusive relationships—a Latina power workbook, by D. A. Nogales. Author, 2010.

Latina power: Utilizando sus 7 fortalezas para decir no al maltrato-manual de trabajo de Latina power, by D. A. Nogales. Author, 2011.

National Latin@ Network website. http://www.nationallatinonetwork.org/

No more secrets: A therapist's guide to group work with adult survivors of domestic violence, by Denise Grant and Irene Lebbad. Bloomington, IN: Balboa Press, 2015.

Week 7: Self-Reflection Drawing or Writing Activity: Current Relationship

Draw a picture of how you view your current relationship.

Goal. Participants reflect and analyze their current relationship.

Instructions. Participants draw a picture of themselves, and they write or draw how they view their current relationship. Participants write or draw positive or negative characteristics of their relationship. Activity time: 10–15 minutes. (See Figures 5.33–5.36).

How do I view my relationship?

[Draw Here]

Are there negative things I don't like?
Are there positive things I like?

FIGURE 5.33   Week 7: Sample Self-Reflection Drawing or Writing Activity

Draw a picture of how you view your current relationship

How do I view my relationship?

Are there negative things I don't like?
Are there positive things I like?

FIGURE 5.34   Week 7: Sample Self-Reflection Drawing or Writing Handout

Draw a picture of how you view your current relationship

¿Cómo veo mi relación?

[Dibuja Aqui]

¿Hay cosas negativas que no me gustan?
¿Hay cosas positivas que me gustan?

FIGURE 5.35   Semana 7: Ejemplo de auto reflexión—Ilustrar o detallar una actividad

Dibuja un cuadro de cómo tu ves tu relación actual

¿Cómo veo mi relación?

¿Hay cosas negativas que no me gustan?
¿Hay cosas positivas que me gustan?

FIGURE 5.36 Semana 7: Ejemplo de auto reflexión—Ilustrar o escribir en el folleto

Dibuja un cuadro de cómo tu ves tusu relación actual

Week 7: Sample Review Handout
Empowerment Group; Date_____

Week 7: Healthy Relationships

Characteristics of healthy relationships. Mutual respect, equality, good communication, no verbal abuse, speaking with "I" statements, support. Person feels loved and respected.

Characteristics of unhealthy relationships. Name calling, disrespectful, aggressive, and unsupportive with work or educational activities. Person does not think about your well-being.

Book recommendation in class. *The Five Love Languages: The Secret to Love That Lasts,* by Gary Chapman (Chicago: Moody, 2010). Provides an understanding of different love languages among individuals.

THINKING EXERCISES

1. Is my relationship healthy?

_____

_____

_____

_____

_____

2. Can I act, think, or feel different? Can I do something different in my relationship?

_____

_____

_____

_____

_____

Week 8: Domestic Violence

Review handout. Pass out review handout from Week 7. Discuss with participants briefly the topic area from the previous week. Encourage participants to do the thinking exercises in between classes.

Objectives.
1. Participants learn the DV Equality Wheel and the Power and Control Wheel.
2. Participants learn safety planning and how to examine lethality in relationships.
3. Participants learn legal aspects of DV such as when to call the police, orders of protection, and basic rights of individuals.
4. Participants learn how to access resources in the community (e.g., shelters or counseling services).

Reading activity. No drawing self-reflection drawing or writing activity. Participants read out loud Appendices E and F handouts, the Equality Wheel and Power and Control Wheel handouts. The Equality Wheel and Power and Control Wheel handouts originated from the Domestic Abuse Intervention Project in 1984 in Duluth, Minnesota.[25] The wheels were developed by victims of DV who participated in the program. Currently, the wheels have been translated into 40 languages and are used in different countries around the world. Participants can choose to pass and not read if they are not comfortable with it.

Teaching and instruction. Pass out the Equality Wheel and Power and Control Wheels and the Safety Planning handout found in Appendix G[26] and the Mental Health/DV Resource handout. Teach on the dynamics, definition, types, and prevalence rates of DV. Discuss the importance of safety, safety planning, legal issues, and lethal situations. Use the Equality Wheel and Power and Control Wheel to teach and have discussion. Discuss the challenges with leaving a DV-related committed relationship. Address the challenges (e.g., immigration status and language) immigrant Latina women face in DV-related relationships within a cultural perspective.

Create a review handout after each class. After class, write a summary of the comments and statements made by the participants in the group. The following week, give the participants the review handout that includes two to three reflection questions that they can do on their own in between classes.

Background information on domestic violence. The term *domestic violence* has multiple definitions, and it has changed over time based on the political climate in the United States and other countries around the world (Kurz, 1989; Walker, 2002).[27] The U.S. government and governments in other countries define DV as abuse that occurs within the context of relationships that features patterns of types of abuse (e.g., sexual, rape, emotional, physical, verbal, stalking, financial) and that includes notions of power and control and in which victims experience isolation (Black et al., 2011).[28] The definition of DV has evolved within the past 30 years as researchers in different disciplines examine the causes of why DV occurs between two people. The majority of the literature on DV explores violence against women by men in heterosexual relationships The National Center for Injury Prevention and Control, Centers for Disease Control and Prevention special report titled *National Intimate Partner and Sexual Violence Survey* (Black et al., 2011)[29] reported that more than 1 in 3 women in the U.S. (35.6%) experienced physical violence, rape, and/or stalking, and, nearly 1 in 10 women (9.4%) experienced raped by an intimate partner in their lifetime. Furthermore, an estimated 16.9% of women experienced sexual violence other than rape (Black et al., 2011). Within the past decade, researchers have also addressed violence against men by women, violence within same-sex intimate relationships, and violence against specifically women of color (Black et al., 2011).[30]

Additional suggested readings for group facilitators.

Boundaries in dating: How healthy choices grow healthy relationships, by Henry Cloud and John Townsend. Grand Rapids, MI: Zondervan, 2000.

Invisible violence: Special issues in intimate partner violence among Latino families living in the U.S., by Joanna Morse. Saarbrücken, Germany: Lambert Academic, 2009.

Latina power: Using your 7 strengths to say no to abusive relationships—a Latina power workbook, by D. A. Nogales. Author, 2010.

Latina power: Utilizando sus 7 fortalezas para decir no al maltrato-manual de trabajo de Latina power, by D. A. Nogales. Author, 2011.

National Latin@ Network website. http://www.nationallatinonetwork.org/

No more secrets: A therapist's guide to group work with adult survivors of domestic violence, by Denise Grant and Irene Lebbad. Bloomington, IN: Baloa Press, 2015.

Additional resources: Legal services websites.

Legal Momentum Advancing Women's Rights. (2005). *Public benefits access for battered immigrant women and children.* Retrieved from National Online Resource Center on Violence: http://www.vawnet.org/summary.php?doc_id=1605&find_type=web_sum_GC

U.S. Department of Justice. (2015). *Application for cancellation of removal and adjustment of status for certain nonpermanent residents.* Retrieved October 29, 2015, from Executive Office for Immigration Review: http://www.justice.gov/sites/default/files/pages/attachments/2015/07/24/eoir42b.pdf.

Week 8: Sample Review Handout

Empowerment Group; Date_____

Week 8: Domestic Violence

Review of domestic violence. A relationship that involves domestic violence is based on power and control. The person wants to dominate and control the other person. Forms of DV include verbal abuse or name calling, physical abuse, sexual abuse, isolation, manipulation, and economic abuse.

Challenges in relationships. The importance of remaining safe in relationships that might be DV-related. Each participant has her own experience, and respecting decisions is important. Often, it is challenging to leave a committed relationship. Why is it difficult to separate?

THINKING EXERCISES

1. Do I have a relationship based on equality or power and control? How do I know which one?

_____

_____

_____

_____

_____

2. How can I remain safe in my current relationship?

_____

_____

_____

_____

_____

PART III: IMPACT OF FACTORS ON RELATIONSHIPS

Week 9: Factors Influencing Relationships

Review handout. Pass out review handout from Week 8. Discuss with participants briefly the topic area from the previous week. Encourage participants to do the thinking exercises in between classes.

Objectives.

1. Participants learn how types of factors (e.g., media, television, Internet and social media sites, religious institutions/religious beliefs, and parental figures) influence current relationships or attitudes about relationships.
2. Participants reflect and analyze how these factors impact relationships.
3. Participants discuss religious institutions (e.g., the Catholic Church or other Christian churches) and the influence of religious beliefs and values on relationships.

Self-reflection drawing or writing activity. Participants draw types of factors (media, television, Internet, and social media sites, religious institutions/religious beliefs, and parental figures), and they write or draw positive or negative factors that influence current relationships.

Teaching and instruction. Discuss the impact of factors on current romantic relationships. Discuss the impact of the media/television, Internet/social media sites, religious values, and parental figures on romantic relationships.

Create a review handout after each class. After class, write a summary of the comments and statements made by the participants in the group. The following week, give the participants the review handout that includes two to three reflection questions that they can do on their own in between classes.

Background information on religious factors. An important factor influencing immigrant Latina women's understanding of relationships is religious institutions, in particular, the Catholic Church and other Christian churches. Immigrant Latina women are influenced by the teachings of the Catholic Church on marriage and romantic relationships and often turn to the Catholic Church for support on issues related to DV (Marrs Fuchsel, 2012).[31] Unfortunately, many immigrant Latina women are not aware of the DV document from the U.S. Bishops. The Catholic Church has taken a formal stand on DV and strongly states that DV in marriage is never justified, is a sin, and is often a crime (U.S. Conference of Bishops, 2002).[32] Immigrant Latina women often are not aware about the process of annulments and the possibility to remarry in the Catholic Church. It is important to examine the Catholic Church and other Christian churches as a factor because church teachings on DV influence immigrant Latina women's understanding of how they view current romantic relationships and ability to make decisions about current romantic relationships.

Additional suggested readings for group facilitators.

Counseling and family therapy with Latino populations: Strategies that work, by Robert Smith and R. Esteban Montilla. New York: Routledge 2015.

Grief therapy with Latinos: Integrating culture for clinicians, by Carmen Iona Vazquez and Dinelia Rosa. New York: Springer, 2011.

Latino families in therapy (2nd ed.), by Celia Jaes Falicov. Guilford family therapy series. New York: Guilford Press, 2015.

Week 9: Alternate Topic: Sexual Abuse

Note: The facilitators should check in with the participants in the middle of the program to assess their interest in understanding the dynamics and definition of sexual abuse. If participants are interested in knowing more about sexual abuse and how to speak to their children on the prevention of sexual abuse, the facilitator should use the alternate topic of sexual abuse as opposed to the *Factors Influencing Relationships* session.

Review handout. Pass out review handout from Week 8. Discuss with participants briefly the topic area from the previous week. Encourage participants to do the thinking exercises in between classes.

Objectives.

1. Participants learn the definition and types of childhood sexual abuse (CSA) and sexual assault.
2. Participants learn how to speak with children about intimate body parts and healthy normal sexual development.
3. Participants learn about mandated reporting if participants suspect sexual abuse of a child.

No drawing or writing activity. Participants have a large-group discussion.

Teaching and instruction. Teach the definition and types of CSA. Teach on the prevalence rates of CSA and sexual assault among the Latino population. CSA is any unwanted sexual activity by one person on another, as by the use of threats or coercion (Browne & Finkelhor, 1986).[33] CSA varies in severity, age, and types of abuse. Perpetrators of CSA vary by age and include family members, friends, acquaintances, and strangers (Browne & Finkelhor, 1986).[34] Teach and discuss the difficulties of disclosing incidences of CSA. Discuss the difficulties of managing feelings of shame, anxiety, and confusion. Discuss the challenges of receiving familial support when attempting to disclose incidences of CSA. Discuss the importance of seeking professional help to manage and recover from CSA that influences current adult behavior and relationships.

Teach and discuss how to respond to children who disclose incidences of CSA. The following information on how to speak to children was obtained from the Lumpkin Family Connection: A Community Collaborative (2008)[35] in the report titled *Healthy Childhood Sexual Development and How to Talk to Your Child about Sex and Sexual Abuse*. Discuss the following information with participants on how to speak to children: (a) remember that children are already hearing about sex through the media or other children; (b) develop children's understanding of sexuality when they are young and encourage children to explore their thoughts and feelings about sexuality; (c) stay open and listen carefully to what children disclose; (d) speak directly with correct terms when explaining normal sexual development; and (e) tell children that if anyone touches them in their private areas they must come and speak with the parent—no matter who it is.

Create a review handout after each class. After class, write a summary of the comments and statements made by the participants in the group. The following week, give the participants the review handout that includes two to three reflection questions that they can do on their own in between classes.

Background information on sexual abuse and familism. Low and Organista (2000)[36] reported on *familism* as a source of strength and support to Latina victims of previous sexual assault. On the other hand, *familism* may serve as a deterrent to reporting, because of women's allegiance to the family first (Low & Organista, 2000).[37] Dimensions of *familism*, including support among family members and strong ties between family members, likely contribute to Latina women's experiences with CSA (Ulibarri et al., 2009).[38] For example, *familism* could serve as a barrier if the perpetrator is a father or brother. In these cases, the victim may feel reluctant to disclose to keep family unity among respected family members (Ulibarri et al., 2009)[39] or because of shame and fear of the perpetrator. In addition, *familism* is part of the Latino community, not just immediate family members (Guilamo-Ramos, Bouris, Jaccard, Lesesne, & Ballan, 2009; Marrs Fuchsel, 2013).[40] It is likely that the perpetrator and the victim are well-acquainted with members of the community. Victims may feel reluctant to report types of abuse because they do not want to disrupt family cohesion in the community.

In general, Latina women have lower rates of disclosure (Ahrens, Isas, Rios-Mandel, & Lopez, 2010; Marrs Fuchsel et al., 2012).[41] Thus, the cultural influence of *familism* may contribute to immigrant Latina women's ability to report or not report incidences of CSA. In one of few investigations of cultural influences that affect Latinas' ability to disclose incidences of sexual assault and DV, Ahrens et al. (2010)[42] conducted focus groups with Spanish-speaking Latina women with and without previous exposure to violence. In line with theoretical expectations regarding the sociocultural influence of *familism* for this population, several participants had difficulties disclosing because they did not want to disrupt family harmony. Alternatively, several participants who were mothers indicated that speaking to children about sexual abuse and not allowing daughters to have sleepovers might have prevented a future sexual abuse incident (Ahrens et al., 2010).[43] In another study, Ullman and Filipas (2005)[44] examined race/ethnicity and CSA among 461 women college students. Latina students experienced negative social reactions (i.e., persons reacted with embarrassment/disgust) when attempting to disclose. Although these findings are useful for understanding Latina's general experiences, research that specifically examines CSA and DV among immigrant Latina women is limited. Examining CSA among immigrant Latina women is important because of the low rates of disclosure and the impact on current relationships.

Background information on the correlation between childhood sexual abuse and domestic violence. In the general population of women, evidence suggests that past CSA experiences are risk factors for future DV incidences in relationships (Daigneault, Hébert, & McDuff, 2009; Hattery, 2009; Krebs, Brieding, Browne, & Warner, 2011; Watson & Halford, 2010).[45] Among Norwegian women, women who experienced familial incest in childhood were 25% more likely to experience DV with multiple partners (Karin Barin Bø & Bjørkly, 2008).[46] Furthermore, findings from structured interviews among white and African American women indicated that women who experienced types of CSA (i.e., incest, premature sexual encounters, and childhood prostitution) were at higher risk of experiencing DV in current relationships (Hattery, 2009).[47]

Additional suggested readings for group facilitators.

Counseling and family therapy with Latino populations: Strategies that work, by Robert Smith and R. Esteban Montilla. New York: Routledge, 2015.

Grief therapy with Latinos: Integrating culture for clinicians, by Carmen Iona Vazquez and Dinelia Rosa. New York: Springer, 2011.

Healing the trauma of abuse: A women's workbook, by Maxine Copeland and Mary Ellen Harris. Oakland, CA: New Harbinger, 2000.

Intimate partner sexual violence: A multidisciplinary guide to improving services and support for survivors of rape and abuse, by Louise McOrmond-Plummer, Patricia Easteal, and Jennifer Levy-Peck. London: Jessica Kingsley, 2013.

Latino families in therapy (2nd ed.), by Celia Jaes Falicov. Guilford family therapy series. New York: Guilford Press, 2015.

Trauma recovery and empowerment: A clinician's guide for working with women in groups, by Maxine Harris. New York: Free Press, 1998.

Week 9: Self-Reflection Drawing or Writing Activity: Factors

Factors: Are they positive or negative influences?

Goals. Participants reflect and analyze the types of factors and influences on current romantic relationships.

Instructions. Participants write or draw how factors influence their understanding of current romantic relationships. Participants reflect on positive and negative characteristics of types of factors on romantic relationships. Activity time: 10–15 minutes. (See Figures 5.37–5.40).

FIGURE 5.37 Week 9: Sample Self-Reflection Drawing or Writing Activity
Factors: Are they positive or negative influences?

YES, I CAN (*SÍ, YO PUEDO*)

FIGURE 5.38   Week 9: Sample Self-Reflection Drawing or Writing Handout
Factors: Are they positive or negative influences?

FIGURE 5.39 Semana 9: Ejemplo de auto reflexión—Ilustrar o detallar actividades

Los factores ¿Son influencias positivas o negativas?

FIGURE 5.40   Semana 9: Ejemplo de auto reflexión—Ilustrar o escribir en el folleto

Los factores ¿Son influencias positivas o negativas?

Week 9: Sample Review Handout

Empowerment Group; Date_____

Week 9: Factors Influencing Relationships

Parental figures and religious institutions. Positive influences might include parents are concerned, sincere, loving, and want the best for their children and relationships. Negative influences could include that parents are overprotective; they "do not let you be." Religious persons (e.g., pastors or priests) describe God as a loving God; relationships are based on the love of God, each other, and children. Negative influences could include staying in committed relationships due to religious beliefs despite incidences of DV.

Media, television, Internet, social media sites, and other factors: Negative influences include women are not respected; women are seen as sexual objects on television programs, social media, and the Internet. Other factors include husbands or partners not being faithful and having multiple affairs.

THINKING EXERCISES

1. In my relationship, have I had problems with infidelity?

_____

_____

_____

_____

_____

2. What do I want in my relationship?

_____

_____

_____

_____

_____

Week 9: Sample Alternate Topic Review Handout

Empowerment Group; Date_____

Week 9: Sexual abuse

Review of sexual abuse. Childhood sexual abuse (CSA) varies by severity and age. Believe persons who disclose incidences of CSA. Persons who disclose incidences of CSA may experience different feelings (i.e., shame, embarrassment, guilt, confusion, depression). Professional help is available (e.g., counseling and medical care).

Review of how to respond to children who disclose. Believe children who disclose. Provide support and respond positively when children disclose.

THINKING EXERCISES

1. How do I feel about the topic of sexual abuse?

_____

_____

_____

_____

_____

2. Has someone tried to hurt me in the past? Someone in my family? What can I do to receive help?

_____

_____

_____

_____

_____

Week 10: Talking to Children

Review handout. Pass out review handout from Week 9. Discuss with participants briefly the topic area from the previous week. Encourage participants to do the thinking exercises in between classes.

Objectives.

1. Participants reflect on how to speak with children and adolescents about healthy dating and romantic relationships.
2. Participants learn how to promote self-respect among children and adolescents.
3. Participants learn effective ways to discuss healthy relationships with children and adolescents.

Self-reflection drawing or writing activity. Participants draw a picture of a crystal ball (See Figure 5.41). Participants are asked to imagine speaking to children or adolescence about healthy dating and romantic relationships.

Teaching and instruction. Teach and discuss effective ways to speak with children about healthy dating experiences and relationships.

Create a review handout after each class. After class, write a summary of the comments and statements made by the participants in the group. The following week, give the participants the review handout that includes two to three reflection questions that they can do on their own in between classes.

Background information on speaking to children. It is important for facilitators to review the information from the previous weeks on self-esteem, dating, cultural concepts, healthy relationships, and domestic violence when discussing material on how to speak to children about healthy dating and relationships. For example, facilitators can use the handout on Characteristics of Healthy Relationships (i.e., Week 5, class on dating) to discuss concepts such as mutual respect, honest communication, and individual interests and hobbies. Facilitators should review with participants the previous week's topics as a method of using the information learned to inform their children about healthy dating. A good sense of self also contributes to healthy dating and decision-making ability among children and teenagers. Facilitators should review with participants the class on self-esteem and the importance of having a good sense of self and assessing current self-esteem. By doing so, participants can discuss with their children how they feel about themselves (i.e., self-esteem) and how that might impact dating experiences.

Examination is needed regarding parents' ability to communicate to young girls and boys about what it means to have a family without violence and the impact of parenting stress or other cultural concepts that may influence their ability to communicate to young girls and boys. Edelson, et al. (2007)[48] examined the differences in effects of DV between Latina and non-Latina women. As opposed to non-Latina women, Latina women who had been victims of DV had higher levels of parenting stress due to their child's behavior. Therefore, it is important to examine parental stress and parents' ability to communicate to young girls.

Week 10: Self-Reflection Drawing or Writing Activity: Letter

Draw a picture of a crystal ball and write a letter to your child. What will you say?

Goal: Participants reflect on how to speak to children and adolescents about healthy dating experiences and romantic relationships.

Instructions: Participants draw a crystal ball and they imagine writing a letter or drawing to their children. The participant writes or draws a letter to their child addressing what the participant would hope for their child's future dating experiences. Activity time: 10–15 minutes. (See Figures 5.41–5.44).

What is a healthy relationship?

Dear Child,

Love,
Mom

Crystal Ball

FIGURE 5.41   Week 10: Sample Self-Reflection Drawing or Writing Activity
Draw a picture of a crystal ball and write a letter to your child. What will you say?

What is a healthy relationship?

Crystal Ball

FIGURE 5.42   Week 10: Sample Self-Reflection Drawing or Writing Handout

Draw a picture of a crystal ball and write a letter to your child. What will you say?

¿Qué es una relación sana?

Querido Niño/Niña,

Con amor,
Mama

Bola de Cristal

FIGURE 5.43 Semana 10: Ejemplo de auto reflexión—Ilustrar o detallar una actividad

Dibuja una bola de cristal y escribe una carta para tu niño o niña: ¿Qué le dirías?

¿Qué es una relación sana?

Bola de Cristal

FIGURE 5.44   Semana 10: Ejemplo de auto reflexión—Ilustrar o escribir en el folleto

Dibuja una bola de cristal y escribe una carta para tu niño o niña: ¿Qué le dirías?

Empowerment Group; Date_____

Week 10: Talking to children

Review talking to children. It is important to do self-reflection work on identity and healthy dating and relationship experiences before speaking to children and adolescents. It is important to model for children and adolescents healthy relationships. Husbands or partners who are abusive are encouraged to seek professional help.

THINKING EXERCISES

1. How will I speak to my children/adolescent about healthy relationships?

_____

_____

_____

_____

_____

2. What kind of relationship do I want my child to have?

_____

_____

_____

_____

_____

Week 11: Graduation and Conclusion

Review handout. Pass out review handout from Week 10. Discuss with participants briefly the topic area from the previous week.

Objectives.

1. Participants reflect on their group experience in the 10-week program.
2. Participants discuss next steps and learn about available resources in the community (i.e., professional counseling or other services).
3. Participants reflect on topics and relationships that have been formed and established in the group.

Self-reflection drawing or writing activity. Participants draw or write things that they will take away from the program for future use, like packing a suitcase.

Teaching and instruction. Discuss and review topics in the 10-week program. Discuss the suitcase activity with participants. Discuss what they learned and what they will take away from participating in the program. Discuss different resources in the community. The Mental Health/DV Resource handout should be distributed one more time. Participants receive graduation certificates and a celebratory meal is provided. If the agency has monetary funds available, gifts bags that include a journal (i.e., an important item so the participants can continue writing or drawing), pen, and chocolates should be distributed to the participants for participating in the program.

Setting up the last session. Facilitators should decorate the room, as the last class is a celebratory experience. The use of streamers and balloons is appropriate. If participants agree, a group picture should be taken that can be sent to the participants as a remembrance of the group experience and completion of the program.

Week 11: Self-Reflection Drawing or Writing Activity: Suitcase Activity

"What will you take with you?"

Goal: Participants reflect on their experiences in the SYP program. Participants describe what they learned from each other and from the group facilitator, if any changes occurred, and what they hope to take with them upon completion of the SYP program.

Instructions: Participants draw a suitcase (See Figure 5.45) and they write or draw about their experiences and what they learned in the SYP program. Participants write or draw new ideas, any changes, new experiences and feelings they might have gained and that they will take with them. Activity time: 10–15 minutes. (See Figures 5.45–5.49).

What am I taking with me?

- Courage
- New Experiences
- Friends
- Knowledge
- What is a healthy relationship

FIGURE 5.45 Week 11: Sample Self-Reflection Drawing or Writing Activity
Suitcase Activity: "What will you take with you?"

What am I taking with me?

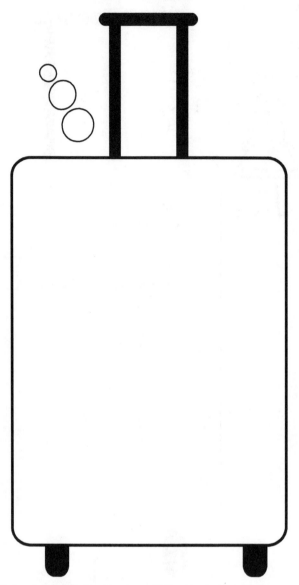

FIGURE 5.46   Week 11: Sample Self-Reflection Drawing or Writing Handout Suitcase Activity, "What will you take with you?"

¿Qué cosas estoy llevando conmigo?

- Valor
- Nueva Experiencia
- Amigos
- Conocimiento
- Que es una relación sana

FIGURE 5.47   Semana 11: Ejemplo de auto reflexión—Ilustrar o detallar una actividad
Maleta de actividades, ¿Qué llevarías contigo?

¿Qué cosas estoy llevando conmigo?

FIGURE 5.48   Semana 11: Ejemplo de auto reflexión—Ilustrar o escribir en el folleto
Maleta de actividades, ¿Qué llevarías contigo?

Empowerment Group for Women
Superacion Personal: Grupo Para Mujeres

This Certificate is awarded to

_____
Name of Recipient

CERTIFICATE OF COMPLETION AND GRADUATION

Completed 11 Weeks, 2 Hours per Week

_____
Name of Facilitator

_____
Date

FIGURE 5.49 Graduation Certificate

NOTES

1. Cast, A. D., & Burke, P. J. (2002). A theory of self esteem. *Social Forces, 80,* 1041–1068. doi:10.1353/sof.2002.0003

2. Ibid.

3. Aranda, M. P., Castaneda, I., Lee, P. J., & Sobel, E. (2001). Stress, social support, and coping as predictors of depressive symptoms: Gender differences among Mexican Americans. *Social Work Research, 1,* 37–48. doi:10.1093/swr/25.1.37

4. Ibid.

5. Marrs Fuchsel, C., Murphy, S., & Dufresne, R. (2012). Domestic violence, culture, and relationship dynamics among immigrant Mexican women. *Affilia: Journal of Women and Social Work, 27,* 263–274. doi:10.1177/0886109912452403

6. Forte, J. (2007). *Human behavior and the social environment: Models, metaphors, and maps for applying theoretical perspectives to practice.* Belmont, CA: Brooks/Cole.

7. Figley, C. R. (2012). *Encyclopedia of trauma: An interdisciplinary guide.* Thousand Oaks, CA: SAGE; Gorde, M. W., Helfrich, C. A., & Finlayson, M. L. (2004). Trauma symptoms and life skill needs of domestic violence victims. *Journal of Interpersonal Violence, 6,* 691–708. doi:10.1177/0886260504263871; Humphreys, C. & Thiara, R. (2003). Mental health and domestic violence: "I call it symptoms of abuse." *British Journal of Social Work, 33,* 209–226. doi:10.1093/bjsw/33.2.209

8. Figley, C. R. (2012). *Encyclopedia of trauma: An interdisciplinary guide.* Thousand Oaks, CA: SAGE; Gorde, M. W., Helfrich, C. A., & Finlayson, M. L. (2004). Trauma symptoms and life skill needs of domestic violence victims. *Journal of Interpersonal Violence, 6,* 691–708. doi:10.1177/0886260504263871

9. National Center on Domestic and Sexual Violence. (2013a). *Teen equality wheel* (Spanish and English). Retrieved May 22, 2013, from http://www.ncdsv.org/publications_wheel.html; National Center on Domestic and Sexual Violence (2013b). *Teen power and control wheel* (Spanish and English). Retrieved May 22, 2013, from http://www.ncdsv.org/publications_wheel.html

10. Umaña-Taylor, A. J., & Fine, M. A. (2003). Predicting commitment to wed among Hispanic and Anglo partners. *Journal of Marriage and Family, 65,* 117–139. doi:10.1111/j.1741-3737.2003.00117.x

11. Ulloa, E. O., Jaycox, L. H., Skinner, S. K., & Orsburn, M. M. (2008). Attitudes about violence and dating among Latino/a boys and girls. *Journal of Ethnic and Cultural Diversity, 17,* 157–176. doi:10.1080/15313200801941721

12. McGoldrick, M., Gerson, R., & Petry, S. (2008). *Genograms: Assessment and intervention* (3rd ed.). New York: W. W. Norton.

13. Brabeck, K. M., & Guzmán, M. R. (2009). Exploring Mexican-origin intimate partner abuse survivors' help-seeking within their sociocultural contexts. *Violence and Victims, 24,* 817–832. doi:10.1891/0886-6708.24.6.817; Klevens, J., Shelley, G., Clavel-Arcas, C., Barney, D. D., Tobar, C., Duran, E. S., Barajas Mazaheri, R., & Esparza, J. (2007). Latinos' perspectives and experiences with intimate partner violence. *Violence Against Women, 13,* 141–158. doi:10.1177/1077801206296980; Vidales, G. T. (2010). Arrested justice: The multifaceted plight of immigrant Latinas who faced domestic violence. *Journal of Family Violence, 25,* 533–544. doi:10.1007/s10896-010-93095

14. Brabeck, K. M., & Guzmán, M. R. (2009). Exploring Mexican-origin intimate partner abuse survivors' help-seeking within their sociocultural contexts. *Violence and Victims, 24,* 817–832. doi:10.1891/0886-6708.24.6.817

15. Marrs Fuchsel, C., Murphy, S., & Dufresne, R. (2012). Domestic violence, culture, and relationship dynamics among immigrant Mexican women. *Affilia: Journal of Women and Social Work, 27,* 263–274. doi:10.1177/0886109912452403

16. Vidales, G. T. (2010). Arrested justice: The multifaceted plight of immigrant Latinas who faced domestic violence. *Journal of Family Violence, 25,* 533–544. doi:10.1007/s10896-010-93095

17. Kulkarni, S. (2007). Romance narrative, feminine ideals, and developmental detours for young mothers. *Affilia: Journal of Women and Social Work, 22,* 9–22. doi:10.1177/0886109906295765

18. Arizona Coalition Against Domestic Violence. (2002). *Characteristics of healthy relationships* [Domestic violence training handout]. Phoenix, AZ: Np.

19. Antle, B. F., Karam, E., Christensen, D. N., Barbee, A. P., & Sar, B. K. (2011). An evaluation of healthy relationship education to reduce intimate partner violence. *Journal of Family Social Work, 14*, 387–406. doi:10.1080/10522158.2011.616482; Beck, L. & Clark, M. S. (2010). What constitutes a healthy communal marriage and why relationship stage matters. *Journal of Family Theory & Review, 2*, 299–315. doi:10.111/j.1756-2589.2010.00063.x; Young, C. (2004). Healthy relationships: Where's the research? *The Family Journal: Counseling and Therapy for Couples and Families, 2*, 159–162. doi:10.1177/1066480703262090

20. Young, C. (2004). Healthy relationships: Where's the research? *The Family Journal: Counseling and Therapy for Couples and Families, 2*, 159–162. doi:10.1177/1066480703262090

21. Ibid.

22. Ibid.

23. Ibid.

24. Ibid.

25. Home of the Duluth Model: Social Change to End Violence Against Women. (1984). *Equality wheel*. Retrieved May 22, 2013, from http://www.theduluthmodel.org/training/wheels.html; Home of the Duluth Model: Social Change to End Violence Against Women. (1984). *Power and control wheel*. Retrieved May 22, 2013, from http://www.theduluthmodel.org/training/wheels.html

26. National Center on Domestic and Sexual Violence. (2013a). *Domestic violence personalized safety plan*. Retrieved May 22, 2013, from http://www.ncdsv.org/publications_safetyplans.html

27. Kurz, D. (1989). Social science perspectives on wife abuse: Current debates and future directions. *Gender & Society, 3*, 489–505; Walker, L. E. (2002). The politics of trauma practice: Politics, psychology and the battered woman's movement. *Journal of Trauma Practice, 1*, 81–102.

28. Black, M. C., Basile, K. C., Breiding, M. J., Smith, S. G., Walters, M. L., Merrick, M. T., Chen, J., & Stevens, M. R. (2011). *The National Intimate Partner and Sexual Violence Survey (NISVS): 2010 Summary Report*. Atlanta, GA: National Center for Injury Prevention and Control, Centers for Disease Control and Prevention.

29. Ibid.

30. Ibid.

31. Marrs Fuchsel, C. (2012). The Catholic Church as a support for immigrant Mexican women living with domestic violence. *Social Work & Christianity, 39*(1), 66–87.

32. U.S. Conference of Catholic Bishops. (2002). *When I call for help: A pastoral response to domestic violence against women*. Retrieved July 13, 2010, from http://www.usccb.org/laity/help.htm

33. Brown, A., & Finkelhor, D. (1986). Impact of child sexual abuse: A review of the research. *Psychological Bulletin, 99*, 66–77. doi:10.1037//0033-2909.99.1.66

34. Ibid.

35. Lumpkin Family Connection: A Community Collaborative. (2008). *Healthy childhood sexual development and how to talk to your child about sex and sexual abuse*. Retrieved May 22, 2013, from http://www.lumpkin.k12.ga.us/~fc/lumpkin_family_connection/parent_resources.html

36. Low, G., & Organista, K. C. (2000). Latinas and sexual assault: Toward culturally sensitive assessment and intervention. *Journal of Multicultural Social Work, 8*, 131–157. doi:10.1300/J285v08n01_06

37. Ibid.

38. Ulibarri, M. D., Ulloa, E. C., & Camacho, L. (2009). Prevalence of sexually abusive experiences in childhood and adolescence among a community sample of Latinas: A descriptive study. *Journal of Child Sexual Abuse, 18*, 405–421. doi:10.1080/10538710903051088

39. Ibid.

40. Guilamo-Ramos, V., Bouris, A., Jaccard, J., Lesesne, C., & Ballan, M. (2009). Familial and cultural influences on sexual risk behaviors among Mexican, Puerto Rican, and Dominican youth. *AIDS Education and Prevention, 21*, 61–79. doi:10.1521/aeap.2009.21.5_supp.61; Marrs Fuchsel, C. (2013). *Familism, sexual abuse, and domestic violence among immigrant

Mexican women. *Affilia: Journal of Women and Social Work, 28*, 378–389. doi:10.1177/0886109913503265

41. Ahrens, C. E., Isas, L., Rios-Mandel, L. C., & Lopez, M. (2010). Talking about interpersonal violence: Cultural influences on Latinas' identification and disclosure of sexual assault and intimate partner violence. *Psychological Trauma: Theory, Research, Practice, and Policy, 2*, 284–295. doi:10.1037/a0018605; Marrs Fuchsel, C., Murphy, S., & Dufresne, R. (2012). Domestic violence, culture, and relationship dynamics among immigrant Mexican women. *Affilia: Journal of Women and Social Work, 27*, 263–274. doi:10.1177/0886109912452403

42. Ahrens, C. E., Isas, L., Rios-Mandel, L. C., & Lopez, M. (2010). Talking about interpersonal violence: Cultural influences on Latinas' identification and disclosure of sexual assault and intimate partner violence. *Psychological Trauma: Theory, Research, Practice, and Policy, 2*, 284–295. doi:10.1037/a0018605

43. Ibid.

44. Ullman, S. E., & Filipas, H. H. (2005). Ethnicity and child sexual abuse experiences of female college students. *Journal of Child Sexual Abuse, 14*, 67–89. doi:10.1300/J070v14n03_04

45. Daigneault, I., Hébert, M., & McDuff, P. (2009). Men's and women's childhood sexual abuse and victimization in adult partner relationships: A study of risk factors. *Child Abuse and Neglect: The International Journal, 33*, 638–647. doi:10.1016/j.chiabu.2009.04.003; Hattery, A. J. (2009). Sexual abuse in childhood and adolescence and intimate partner violence in adulthood among African American and white women. *Race, Gender, & Class, 16*, 193–217; Krebs, C., Brieding, M. J., Browne, A., & Warner, T. (2011). The association between different types of intimate partner violence experienced by women. *Journal of Family Violence, 26*, 487–500. doi:10.1007/s10896-011-9383-3; Watson, B., & Halford, W. K. (2010). Classes of childhood sexual abuse and women's adult couple relationships. *Violence and Victims, 25*, 518–535. doi:10.1007/s10567-010-0066-z

46. Karin Bø Vatnar, S. & Bjørkly, S. (2008). An interactional perspective of intimate partner violence: An in-depth semi-structured interview of a representative sample of help-seeking women. *Journal of Family Violence, 23*, 265–279. doi:10.1007/s10896-007-9150-7

47. Hattery, A. J. (2009). Sexual abuse in childhood and adolescence and intimate partner violence in adulthood among African American and white women. *Race, Gender, & Class, 16*, 193–217.

48. Edelson, M. G., Hokoda, A., & Ramos-Lira, L. (2007). Differences in effects of domestic violence between Latina and Non-Latina women. *Journal of Family Violence, 22*, 1–10. doi:10.1007/s10896-006-9051-1

FURTHER READING

Ahmed, S. M., Beck, B, Maurana, C. A, & Newton, G. (2004). Overcoming barriers to effective community-based participatory research in U.S. medical schools. *Education for Health, 17*(2), 141–151. doi:10.1080/13576280410001710969

Ahrens, C. E., Isas, L., Rios-Mandel, L. C., & Lopez, M. (2010). Talking about interpersonal violence: Cultural influences on Latinas' identification and disclosure of sexual assault and intimate partner violence. *Psychological Trauma: Theory, Research, Practice, and Policy, 2,* 284–295. doi:10.1037/a0018605

Ahrens, C. E., Isas, L., & Viveros, M. (2011). Enhancing Latinas' participation in research on sexual assault: Cultural considerations in the design and implementation of research in the Latino community. *Violence Against Women, 17,* 177–188. doi:10.1177/1077801210397701

Alcalde, M. C. (2010). Violence across borders: Familism, hegemonic masculinity, and self-sacrificing femininity in the lives of Mexican and Peruvian migrant. *Latino Studies, 8*(1), 48–68. doi:10.1057/lst.2009.44

Allen, K. N., & Wozniak, D. F. (2011). The language of healing: Women's voices in healing and recovering from domestic violence. *Social Work in Mental Health, 9,* 37–55. doi:10.1080/15332985.2010.494540

American Psychiatric Association. (2013). *Diagnostic and statistical manual of mental disorders* (5th ed.). Arlington, VA: American Psychiatric Association.

Antle, B. F., Karam, E., Christensen, D. N., Barbee, A. P., & Sar, B. K. (2011). An evaluation of healthy relationship education to reduce intimate partner violence. *Journal of Family Social Work, 14,* 387–406. doi:10.1080/10522158.2011.616482

Aranda, M. P., Castaneda, I., Lee, P. J., & Sobel, E. (2001). Stress, social support, and coping as predictors of depressive symptoms: Gender differences among Mexican Americans. *Social Work Research, 1,* 37–48. doi:10.1093/swr/25.1.37

Arizona Coalition Against Domestic Violence. (2002). *Characteristics of healthy relationships* [Domestic violence training handout]. Phoenix, AZ: Np.

Baker, C. K., Cook, S. L., & Norris, F. H. (2003). Domestic violence and housing problems: A contextual analysis of women's help-seeking, received informal support, and formal system response. *Violence Against Women, 9,* 754–783. doi:10.1177/1077801203009007002

Ball, B., Tharp, A. T., Noonan, R. K., Valle, L. A., Hamburger, M. E., & Rosenbluth, B. (2012). Expect Respect support group: Preliminary evaluation of a dating violence prevention program for at-risk youth. *Violence Against Women, 18,* 746–762. doi:10.1177/1077801212455188

Basile, K. C., Chen, J., Black, M. C., & Saltzman, L. E. (2007). Prevalence and characteristics of sexual violence victimization among U.S. adults, 2001-2003. *Violence and Victims, 22,* 437–448. doi:10.1891/088667007781553955

Beck, J. S. (2011). *Cognitive therapy: Basics and beyond.* (2nd Ed.) Guilford Press: New York.

Beck, L. & Clark, M. S. (2010). What constitutes a healthy communal marriage and why relationship stage matters. *Journal of Family Theory & Review, 2,* 299–315. doi:10.111/j.1756-2589.2010.00063.x

Bent-Goodley, T. B., & Fowler, D. N. (2006). Spiritual and religious abuse: Expanding what is known about domestic violence. *Affilia: Journal of Women and Social Work, 21,* 282–295. doi:10.1177/0886109906288901

Berg, B. L. (2009). *Qualitative research methods for the social sciences.* (7th Ed.). Boston, MA: Allyn & Bacon.

Bhuyan, R., & Velagapudi, K. (2013). From one "Dragon Sleigh" to another: Advocating for immigrant women facing violence in Kansas. *Affilia: Journal of Women and Social Work, 28,* 65–78. doi:10.1177/0886109912475049

Black, M. C., Basile, K. C., Breiding, M. J., Smith, S. G., Walters, M. L., Merrick, M. T., Chen, J., & Stevens, M. R. (2011). *The National Intimate Partner and Sexual Violence Survey (NISVS): 2010 Summary Report.* Atlanta, GA: National Center for Injury Prevention and Control, Centers for Disease Control and Prevention.

Bowlby, J. (1988). Developmental psychiatry comes of age. *The American Journal of Psychiatry, 1,* 1–9.

Brabeck, K. M., & Guzman, M. R. (2008). Frequency and perceived effectiveness of strategies to survive abuse employed by battered Mexican-origin women. *Violence Against Women, 14,* 1274–1294. doi:10.1177/1077801208325087

Brabeck, K. M., & Guzmán, M. R. (2009). Exploring Mexican-origin intimate partner abuse survivors' help-seeking within their sociocultural contexts. *Violence and Victims, 24,* 817–832. doi:10.1891/0886-6708.24.6.817

Brizendine, L. (2007). *The female brain.* Redondo Beach, CA: Morgan Road Books.

Broder, T. (2005). Immigrant eligibility for public benefits. In *Immigration & nationality law handbook* (pp. 759–782). Washington, DC: American Immigration Lawyers Association.

Brown, A., & Finkelhor, D. (1986). Impact of child sexual abuse: A review of the research. *Psychological Bulletin, 99,* 66–77. doi:10.1037//0033-2909.99.1.66

Cabassa, L (2002). Measuring acculturation: Where we are and where we need to go. *Hispanic Journal of Behavioral Sciences, 25,* 127–146. doi:10.1177/0739986303253626

Cachelin, F. M., Schug, R. A., Juarez, L. C., & Monreal, T. K. (2005). Sexual abuse and eating disorders in a community sample of Mexican American women. *Hispanic Journal of Behavioral Sciences, 27,* 533–546. doi:10.1177/0739986305279022

Campbell, W. S. (2008). Lessons in resilience: Undocumented Mexican women in South Carolina. *Affilia: Journal of Women and Social Work, 23,* 231–241. doi:10.1177/0886109908319172

Casey, E. A. & Nurius, P. S. (2006). Trends in the prevalence and characteristics of sexual violence: A cohort analysis. *Violence and Victims, 22,* 629–644. doi:10.1891/0886-6708.21.5.629

Cast, A. D., & Burke, P. J. (2002). A theory of self esteem. *Social Forces, 80,* 1041–1068. doi:10.1353/sof.2002.0003

Chapman, G. (2010). *The five love languages: The secret to love that lasts.* Chicago: Moody.

Charter, R. (2003). Study samples are too small to produce sufficiently precise reliability coefficients. *The Journal of General Psychology, 130,* 117–129. doi:10.1080/00221300309601280

City of West Chicago. (2016). Support services division. Retrieved from http://westchicago.org/departments/police/support-services-division/

Cloud, H., & Townsend, J. (2000). *Boundaries in dating: How healthy choices grow healthy relationships.* Grand Rapids, MI: Zondervan.

Cook, S. L., Gidycz, C. A., Koss, M. P., & Murphy, M. (2011). Emerging issues in the measurement of rape victimization. *Violence Against Women, 17,* 201–218. doi:10.1177/1077801210397741

Copel, L. C. (2008). The lived experience of women in abusive relationships who sought spiritual guidance. *Issues in Mental Health Nursing, 29,* 115–130. doi:10.1080/01612840701792365

Copeland, M. E., & Harris, M. (2000). *Healing the trauma of abuse: A women's workbook.* Oakland, CA: New Harbinger.

Cuevas, C. A., Sabina, C., & Bell, K. A. (2012). The effect of acculturation and immigration on the victimization and psychological distress link in a national sample of Latino women. *Journal of Interpersonal Violence, 27*(8), 1428–1456. doi:10.1177/0886260511425797

Cunningham, L. T. (2005). *The effectiveness of domestic violence workshops for Catholic pastoral ministers and implications for practice.* Unpublished doctoral dissertation, Adler School of Professional Psychology, Chicago.

Daigneault, I., Hébert, M., & McDuff, P. (2009). Men's and women's childhood sexual abuse and victimization in adult partner relationships: A study of risk factors. *Child Abuse and Neglect: The International Journal, 33,* 638–647. doi:10.1016/j.chiabu.2009.04.003

Danielson, T., Lucas, P., Malinowski, R., & Pittman, S. (2009). Set free ministries: A comprehensive model for domestic violence congregational interventions. *Social Work & Christianity, 36,* 480–493.

Davis, M., Eshelman, E. R., & McKay, M. (2008). *The relaxation and stress reduction workbook* (New Harbinger self-help workbook). Oakland, CA: New Harbinger.

De los Angeles Cruz-Almanza, M., Gaona-Márquez, L., & Sánchez-Sosa, J. J. (2006). Empowering women abused by their problem drinker spouses: Effects of a cognitive-behavioral intervention. *Salud Mental, 29,* 25–31.

Dobash, R. E., & Dobash, R. P. (1979). *Violence against wives: A case against the patriarchy.* New York: Free Press.

Domínguez, S., & Lubitow, A. (2008). Transnational ties, poverty, and identity: Latin American immigrant women in public housing. *Family Relations*, *57*(4), 419–430. Retrieved from http://www.jstor.org.ezproxy.stthomas.edu/stable/20456807

Dreby, J. (2006). Honor and virtue: Mexican parenting in the transnational context. *Gender & Society*, *20*(1), 32–59. doi:10.1177/0891243205282660

Edelson, M. G., Hokoda, A., & Ramos-Lira, L. (2007). Differences in effects of domestic violence between Latina and Non-Latina women. *Journal of Family Violence*, *22*, 1–10. doi:10.1007/s10896-006-9051-1

Ellison, C. G., Trinitapoli, J. A., Anderson, K. L., & Johnson, B. R. (2007). Race/ethnicity, religious involvement, and domestic violence. *Violence Against Women*, *13*, 1094–1112. doi:10.1177/1077801207308259

Erez, E., Adelman, M., & Gregory, C. (2009). Intersections of immigration and domestic violence: Voices of battered immigrant women. *Feminist Criminology*, *4*, 32–56. doi:10.1177/1557085108325413

Falicov, C. J. (2015). *Latino families in therapy* (2nd ed.). (Guilford family therapy series). New York: Guilford Press.

Figley, C. R. (2012). *Encyclopedia of trauma: An interdisciplinary guide*. Thousand Oaks, CA: SAGE.

Flaskerud, J. H. (1988). Is the Likert scale format culturally biased? *Nursing Research*, *37*, 185–186.

Follette, V. M., Briere, J., Rozelle, D., Hopper, J. W., & Rome, D. I. (2014). *Mindfulness-oriented interventions for trauma: Integrating contemplative practices*. New York: Guilford Press.

Forte, J. (2007). *Human behavior and the social environment: Models, metaphors, and maps for applying theoretical perspectives to practice*. Belmont, CA: Brooks/Cole.

Fowler, D. N., & Hill, H. M. (2004). Social support and spirituality as culturally relevant factors in coping among African American women survivors of partner abuse. *Violence Against Women*, *10*, 1267–1282. doi:10.1177/1077801204269001

Fraser, I., McNutt, L., Clark, C., Williams-Muhammed, D., & Lee, R. (2002). Social or support choices for help with abusive relationships: Perceptions of African-American women. *Journal of Family Violence*, *17*, 363–375.

Frias, S. M., & Angel, R. J. (2005). The risk of partner violence among low-income Hispanic subgroups. *Journal of Marriage and Family*, *67*, 552–564. doi:10.1111/j.1741-3737.2005.00153.x

Furman, R., & Negi, N. J. (2007). Social work practice with transnational Latino populations. *International Social Work*, *50*(1), 107–112. doi:10.1177/0020872807072500

Gaines, S. O. Jr., Marelich, W. D., Bledsoe, K. L., Steers, W. N., Henderson, M. C., Granrose, C. S., . . . Page, M. S. (1997). Links between race/ethnicity and cultural values as mediated by racial/ethnic identity and moderated by gender. *Journal of Personality and Social Psychology*, *72*, 1460–1476. doi:10.1037//0022-3514.72.6.1460

Gelles, R. J., & Straus, M. A. (1988). *Intimate violence*. New York: Simon & Schuster.

Giacomazzi, A. L., & Smithey, M. (2001). Community policing and family violence against women: Lessons learned from a multiagency collaborative. *Criminology and Penology*, *4*, 99–122. doi:10.1177/109861101129197761

Glaser, B. (2001). *The grounded theory perspective: Conceptualization contrasted with description*. Mill Valley, CA: Sociology Press.

Glaser, B., & Strauss, A. (1967). *Discovery of grounded theory*. Chicago: Aldine.

Goldman, M. (1999). The Violence Against Women Act: Meeting its goals in protecting battered immigrant women? *Family and Conciliation Courts Review*, *37*, 375–392. doi:10.1111/j.174-1617.1999.tb01311.x

González-López, G. (2007). "Nunca he dejado de tener terror": Sexual violence in the lives of Mexican immigrant women. In D. A. Segura & P. Zavella (Eds.), *Women and migration in the U.S.-Mexico borderlands: A reader* (pp. 224–246). Durham, NC: Duke University Press.

González-López, G., & Gutmann, M. C. (2005). Machismo. In M. C. Horowitz (Ed.), *The new dictionary of the history of ideas, Vol. 4* (pp. 1328–1330). New York: Charles Scribner's.

Gorde, M. W., Helfrich, C. A., & Finlayson, M. L. (2004). Trauma symptoms and life skill needs of domestic violence victims. *Journal of Interpersonal Violence*, *6*, 691–708. doi:10.1177/0886260504263871

Grant, D., & Lebbad, I. (2015). *No more secrets: A therapist's guide to group work with adult survivors of domestic violence*. Bloomington, IN: Balboa Press.

Green, B. L., Chung, J. Y., Daroowalla, A., Kaltman, S., & DeBenedictis, C. (2006). Evaluating the cultural validity of the stressful life events screening questionnaire. *Violence Against Women, 12,* 1191–1213. doi:10.1177/1077801206294534

Greif, G. L., & Ephross, P. H. (2010). *Group work with populations at risk.* Oxford: Oxford University Press.

Grzywacz, J. G., Rao, P., Gentry, A., Marin, A., & Arcury, T. A. (2009). Acculturation and conflict in Mexican immigrants' intimate partnerships: The role of women's labor force participation. *Violence Against Women, 13,* 1194–1212. doi:10.1177/1077801209345144

Guilamo-Ramos, V., Bouris, A., Jaccard, J., Lesesne, C., & Ballan, M. (2009). Familial and cultural influences on sexual risk behaviors among Mexican, Puerto Rican, and Dominican youth. *AIDS Education and Prevention, 21,* 61–79. doi:10.1521/aeap.2009.21.5_supp.61

Gustafson, A. L. (2005). *Seminarians' response to domestic violence: Sex-role attitudes, just world beliefs, and formal training.* Unpublished doctoral dissertation. Alliant International University, Los Angeles, CA.

Hancock, T. (2007a). Addressing wife abuse in Mexican immigrant couples: Challenges for family social workers. *Journal of Family Social Work, 10,* 31–50. doi:10.1300/J039v10n03_03

Hancock, T. (2007b). Sin papeles: Undocumented Mexicans in rural United States. *Affilia: Journal of Women and Social Work, 22,* 175–184. doi:10.1177/0886109906299048

Hancock, T. U., & Ames, N. (2008). Toward a model for engaging Latino lay ministers in domestic violence intervention. *Families in Society: The Journal of Contemporary Social Services, 89,* 623–630. doi:10.1606/1044-3894.3824

Harris, M. (1998). *Trauma recovery and empowerment: A clinician's guide for working with women in groups.* New York: Free Press.

Hattery, A. J. (2009). Sexual abuse in childhood and adolescence and intimate partner violence in adulthood among African American and white women. *Race, Gender, & Class, 16,* 193–217.

Hill, C. (2007). Responses to domestic violence against women. *Origins: CNS [Catholic News Service] Documentary Service, 36,* 613–614.

Hinson, J. V., Koverola, C., & Morahan, M. (2002). An empirical investigation of the psychological sequelae of childhood sexual abuse in an adult Latina population. *Violence Against Women, 8,* 816–844. doi:10.1177/107780102400388498

Home of the Duluth Model: Social Change to End Violence Against Women. (1984). *Equality wheel.* Retrieved May 22, 2013, from http://www.theduluthmodel.org/training/wheels.html

Home of the Duluth Model: Social Change to End Violence Against Women. (1984). *Power and control wheel.* Retrieved May 22, 2013, from http://www.theduluthmodel.org/training/wheels.html

Homiak, K. B., & Singletary, J. E. (2007). Family violence in congregations: An exploratory study of clergy's needs. *Social Work & Christianity, 34,* 18–46.

Humphreys, C. & Thiara, R. (2003). Mental health and domestic violence: "I call it symptoms of abuse." *British Journal of Social Work, 33,* 209–226. doi:10.1093/bjsw/33.2.209

Karin Bø Vatnar, S. & Bjørkly, S. (2008). An interactional perspective of intimate partner violence: An in-depth semi-structured interview of a representative sample of help-seeking women. *Journal of Family Violence, 23,* 265–279. doi:10.1007/s10896-007-9150-7

Kasturirangan, A. (2008). Empowerment and programs designed to address domestic violence. *Violence Against Women, 14,* 1465–1475. doi:10.1177/1077801208325188

Kasturirangan, A., Krishnan, S., & Riger, S. (2004). The impact of culture and minority status on women's experience of domestic violence. *Trauma, Violence, and Abuse, 5,* 318–332. doi:10.1177/1524838004269487

Katerndahl, D. A., Burge, S. K., Kellogg, N., & Parra, J. M. (2005). Differences in childhood sexual abuse experience between adult Hispanic and Anglo women in a primary care setting. *Journal of Child Sexual Abuse, 14,* 85–95. doi:10.1300/J070v14n02_05

Kawahara, D. M., & Espin, O. M. (2012). *Feminist therapy with Latina women: Personal and social voices* (1st ed.) New York: Routledge.

Kendall-Tackett, K. A., Williams, L. M., & Finkelhor, D. (1993). Impact of sexual abuse on children: A review and synthesis of recent empirical studies. *Psychological Bulletin, 113,* 164–180. doi:10.1037//0033-2909.113.1.164

Klevens, J. (2007). An overview of intimate partner violence among Latinos. *Violence Against Women, 13,* 111–122. doi:10.1177/1077801206296979

Klevens, J., Shelley, G., Clavel-Arcas, C., Barney, D. D., Tobar, C., Duran, E. S., Barajas-Mazaheri, R., & Esparza, J. (2007). Latinos' perspectives and experiences with intimate partner violence. *Violence Against Women, 13,* 141–158. doi:10.1177/1077801206296980

Krebs, C., Brieding, M. J., Browne, A., & Warner, T. (2011). The association between different types of intimate partner violence experienced by women. *Journal of Family Violence, 26,* 487–500. doi:10.1007/s10896-011-9383-3

Kreeft, P. (2001). *Catholic Christianity: A complete catechism on Catholic beliefs based on the Catechism of the Catholic Church.* San Francisco, CA: Ignatius Press.

Kulkarni, S. (2007). Romance narrative, feminine ideals, and developmental detours for young mothers. *Affilia: Journal of Women and Social Work, 22,* 9–22. doi:10.1177/0886109906295765

Kurz, D. (1989). Social science perspectives on wife abuse: Current debates and future directions. *Gender & Society, 3,* 489–505.

Leidy, M. S., Guerra, N. G., & Toro, R. I. (2010). A review of family-based programs to prevent youth violence among Latinos. *Hispanic Journal of Behavioral Sciences, 32,* 5–36. doi:10.1177/0739986309353317

Legal Momentum Advancing Women's Rights. (2005). *Public benefits access for battered immigrant women and children.* Retrieved from National Online Resource Center on Violence Against Women: http://www.vawnet.org/summary.php?doc_id=1605&find_type=web_sum_GC

Lieberman, M., & Golant, M. (2002). Leader behaviors as perceived by cancer patients in professionally directed support groups and outcomes. *Group Dynamics: Theory, Research, and Practice, 6,* 267–276. doi:10.1037//1089-2699.6.4.267

Lira, L. R., Koss, M. P., & Russo, N. F. (1999). Mexican American women's definitions of rape and sexual abuse. *Hispanic Journal of Behavioral Sciences, 21,* 236–265. doi:10.1177/0739986399213004

Low, G., & Organista, K. C. (2000). Latinas and sexual assault: Toward culturally sensitive assessment and intervention. *Journal of Multicultural Social Work, 8,* 131–157. doi:10.1300/J285v08n01_06

Lumpkin Family Connection: A Community Collaborative. (2008). *Healthy childhood sexual development and how to talk to your child about sex and sexual abuse.* Retrieved May 22, 2013, from http://www.lumpkin.k12.ga.us/~fc/lumpkin_family_connection/parent_resources.html

Marotta, J. (2013). *50 mindful steps to self-esteem: Everyday practices for cultivating self-acceptance and self- compassion.* Oakland, CA: New Harbinger.

Marrs Fuchsel, C. (2012). The Catholic Church as a support for immigrant Mexican women living with domestic violence. *Social Work & Christianity, 39*(1), 66–87.

Marrs Fuchsel, C. (2013). *Familism,* sexual abuse, and domestic violence among immigrant Mexican women. *Affilia: Journal of Women and Social Work, 28,* 378–389. doi:10.1177/0886109913503265

Marrs Fuchsel, C. (2014a). Exploratory evaluation of *Sí, Yo Puedo*: A culturally competent empowerment program for immigrant Latina women in group settings. *Social Work with Groups, 37,* 279–296. doi:10.1080/01609513.2014.895921

Marrs Fuchsel, C. (2014b). "Yes, I have changed because I am more sure of myself, I feel stronger with more confidence and strength": Examining the experiences of immigrant Latina women participating in the *Sí, Yo Puedo* curriculum. *Journal of Ethnographic and Qualitative Research, 8,* 161–182.

Marrs Fuchsel, C., & Hysjulien, B. (2013). Exploring a domestic violence intervention curriculum for immigrant Mexican women in a group setting: A pilot study. *Social Work with Groups, 36,* 304–320. doi 10.1080/01609513.2013.767130

Marrs Fuchsel, C., Linares, R., Abugattas, A., Padilla, M., & Hartenberg, L. (2015). *Sí, Yo Puedo:* Latinas examining domestic violence and self. *Affilia: Journal of Women and Social Work, 31,* 219–231. doi:10.1177/0886109915608220

Marrs Fuchsel, C., Murphy, S., & Dufresne, R. (2012). Domestic violence, culture, and relationship dynamics among immigrant Mexican women. *Affilia: Journal of Women and Social Work, 27,* 263–274. doi:10.1177/0886109912452403

Marrs Fuchsel, C., Valencia, R., Stefango, E., Uplegger, M., & Sennes, E. (2016). *Sí, Yo Puedo* curricula and police departments: Educating immigrant Latinas. *Affilia, Journal of Women and Social Work.* Epub May 16, doi:10.1080/01609513.2017.1318329

Marrs, C., (2007). *"For me that was the most important—The family": The meaning of marriage and domestic violence among immigrant Mexican women.* Unpublished doctoral dissertation, Arizona State University, Tempe.

Marsiglia, F. F., Miles, B. W., Dustman, P., & Sills, S. (2002). Ties that protect: An ecological perspective on Latino/a urban pre-adolescent drug use. *Journal of Ethnic and Cultural Diversity in Social Work, 11,* 191–220. doi:10.1300/J051v11n03_03

Maxwell, J. A. (1996). *Qualitative research design: An interactive approach.* Thousand Oaks, CA: SAGE.

McGoldrick, M., Gerson, R., & Petry, S. (2008). *Genograms: Assessment and intervention* (3rd ed.). New York: W. W. Norton.

McMullan, E. C, Carlan, P. E., & Nored, L. S. (2010). Future law enforcement officers and social workers: Perceptions of domestic violence. *Journal of Interpersonal Violence, 25,* 1367–1387. doi:10.1177/0886260509346062.

McOrmond-Plummer, L., Easteal, P., & Levy-Peck, J. Y. (2013). *Intimate partner sexual violence: A multidisciplinary guide to improving services and support for survivors of rape and abuse.* London: Jessica Kingley.

McPhail, B. A., Busch, N. B., Kulkarni, S., & Rice, G. (2007). An integrative feminist model: The evolving feminist perspective on intimate partner violence. *Violence Against Women, 13,* 817–841. doi:10.1177/1077801207302039

Messing, J. T., Becerra, D., Ward-Lasher, A. & Androff, D. K. (2015). Latinas' perceptions of law enforcement: Fear of deportation, crime reporting, and trust in the system. *Affilia: Journal of Women and Social Work, 30,* 328–340. doi:10.1177/0886109915576520

Mills, L. (1996). Empowering battered women transnationally: the case for postmodern interventions. *Social Work, 41*(3), 261–268. Retrieved from http://www.jstor.org.ezproxy.stthomas.edu/stable/23718169

Molina, O., Lawrence, S. A., & Azhar-Miller, A. (2009). Divorcing abused Latina immigrant women's experiences with domestic violence support groups. *Journal of Divorce and Remarriage, 50,* 459–471. doi:10.1080/10502550902970561

Monette, D. R., Sullivan, T. J. & DeJong, C. R. (2014). *Applied social research: Tool for the human services* (9th ed.). Belmont, CA: Brooks/Cole.

Moracco, K. E., Hilton, A., Hodges, K. G., & Frasier, P. Y. (2005). Knowledge and attitudes about intimate partner violence among immigrant Latinos in rural North Carolina: Baseline information and implications for outreach. *Violence Against Women, 11,* 337–352. doi:10.1177/1077801204273296

Morales-Campos, D. Y., Casillas, M., & McCurdy, S. A. (2009). From isolation to connection: Understanding a support group for Hispanic women living with gender-based violence in Houston, Texas. *Journal of Immigrant Minority Health, 11,* 57–65. doi:10.1007/s10903-008-9153-3.

Morse, J. (2009). *Invisible violence: Special issues in intimate partner violence among Latino families living in the U.S.* Saarbrücken, Germany: Lambert Academic.

Mouilso, E. R., Calhoun, K. S., & Gidycz, C. (2011). Effects of participation in a sexual assault risk reduction program on psychological distress following revictimization. *Journal of Interpersonal Violence, 26,* 769–788. doi:10.1177/0886260510365862

Murdaugh, C., Hunt, S., Sowell, R., & Santana, I. (2004). Domestic violence in Hispanics in the Southeastern United States: A survey and needs analysis. *Journal of Family Violence, 19,* 107–115. doi:10.1023/B:JOFV.0000019841.58748.51

Myers, R., & Jacobo, J. (2005). *Violence against women: VAWA's strengths and weaknesses.* Washington, DC: Crime Victims Report.

National Center on Domestic and Sexual Violence. (2013a). *Domestic violence personalized safety plan.* Retrieved May 22, 2013, from http://www.ncdsv.org/publications_safetyplans.html

National Center on Domestic and Sexual Violence (2013b). *Teen equality wheel* (Spanish and English). Retrieved May 22, 2013, from http://www.ncdsv.org/publications_wheel.html

National Center on Domestic and Sexual Violence. (2013c). *Teen power and control wheel* (Spanish and English). Retrieved May 22, 2013, from http://www.ncdsv.org/publications_wheel.html

National Latin@ Network. (n.d.). Retrieved October 28, 2015, from National Latin@ Network: http://www.nationallatinonetwork.org/

Newcomb, M. D., Munoz, D. T., & Carmona, J. V. (2009). Child sexual abuse consequences in community samples of Latino and European American adolescents. *Child Abuse and Neglect*, *33*, 533–544. doi:10.1016/j.chiabu.2008.09.014

Nogales, D. A. (2010). *Latina power: Using your 7 strengths to say no to abusive relationships—A Latina power workbook*. Author.

Nogales, D. A. (2011). *Latina power: Utilizando sus 7 fortalezas para decir no al maltrato—Manual de trabajo de Latina power*. Author.

Orloff, L. E., & Kaguyutan, J. V. (2002). Offering a helping hand: Legal protections for battered immigrant women: A history of legislative responses. *American University Journal of Gender Social Policy and Law*, *10*(1), 95–170. Retrieved from http://digitalcommons.wcl.american.edu/cgi/viewcontent.cgi?article=1432&context=jgsp

Parmley, A. M. (2004). Violence against women research post VAWA, where have we been, where are we going? *Violence Against Women*, *10*, 1417–1430. doi:10.1177/1077801204270682

Perilla, J. L. (1999). Domestic violence as a human rights issue: The case of immigrant Latinos. *Hispanic Journal of Behavioral Sciences*, *21*, 107–133. doi:10.1177/0739986399212001

Perilla, J. L., Frndak, K., Lillard, D., & East, C. (2003). A working analysis of women's use of violence in the context of learning, opportunity, and choice. *Violence Against Women*, *9*, 10–46.

Perilla, J. L., Serrata, J. V., Weinberg, J. & Lippy, C. (2012). Integrating women's voices and theory: A comprehensive domestic violence intervention for Latinas. *Women and Therapy*, *35*, 93–105. doi:10.1080/02703149.2012.634731

Pence, E. (2001). Advocacy on behalf of battered women. In C. M. Renzetti, J. L. Edleson, & R. K. Bergen (Eds.), *Sourcebook on violence against women* (pp. 329–343). Thousand Oaks, CA: SAGE.

Perez, S., Johnson, D. M., Wright, C. V. (2012). The attenuating effect of empowerment on IPV-related PTSD symptoms in battered women living in domestic violence shelters. *Violence Against Women*, *11*, 102–117. doi:10.1177/1077801212437348

Petersen, E. (2009). Addressing domestic violence: Challenges experienced by Anglican clergy in the diocese of Cape Town, South Africa. *Social Work & Christianity*, *36*, 449–469.

Pitts, K. M. (2014). Latina immigrants, interpersonal violence, and the decision to report to police. *Journal of Interpersonal Violence*, *29*, 1661–1678. doi:10.1177/0886260513511700

Potter, H. (2007). Battered black women's use of religious services and spirituality for assistance in leaving abusive relationships. *Violence Against Women*, *13*, 262–284. doi:10.1177/1077801206297438

Pyles, L. (2007). The complexities of the religious response to domestic violence: Implications for faith-based initiatives. *Affilia: Journal of Women and Social Work*, *22*, 281–291. doi:10.1177/0886109907302271

Raj, A., & Silverman, J. (2002). Violence against immigrant women: the roles of culture, context, and legal immigrant status on intimate partner violence. *Violence Against Women*, *8*(3), 367–398. doi:10.1177/10778010222183107

Rand, M. (2008). *Criminal victimization*. Washington, DC: U.S. Department of Justice, Bureau of Justice Statistics. Retrieved September 1, 2009, from http://www.ojp.usdoj.gov/bjs/pub/pdf/cv08.pdf

Reina, A. S., & Lohman, B. J. (2015). Barriers preventing Latina immigrants from seeking advocacy services for domestic violence victims: A qualitative analysis. *Journal of Family Violence*, *30*, 479–488. doi:10.1007/s10896-015-9696-8

Reina, A. S., Lohman, B. J., & Maldonado, M. M. (2014). "He said they'd deport me": Factors influencing domestic violence help-seeking practices among Latina immigrants. *Journal of Interpersonal Violence*, *29*(4), 593–615. doi:10.1177/0886260513505214

Rennison, C. M. (2003). *Intimate partner violence and age of victim, 1993–1999*: Bureau of Justice Statistics Special Report. Washington, DC: U.S. Department of Justice Office of Justice Programs.

Resnick, M. (2000). Resilience and protective factors in the lives of adolescents. *Journal of Adolescent Health*, *27*, 1–2. doi:10.1016/S1054-139X(00)00142-7

Reuland, M., Schaefer Morabito, M., Preston, C., & Cheney, J. (2006). Police-community partnerships to address domestic violence. U.S. Department of Justice, Office of Community

Oriented Policing Services. Retrieved from http://ric-zai- inc.com/Publications/cops-p091-pub.pdf

Robbins, R., Tonemah, S., & Robbins, S. (2002). Project eagle: Techniques for multi-family psycho-educational group. *American Indian and Alaska Native Mental Health Research, 10,* 56–74. doi:10.5820/aian.1003.2002.56

Robins, W., Hendin, H. M., & Trzesniewski, K. H. (2001). Measuring global self-esteem: Construct validation of a single-item measure and the Rosenberg Self-Esteem Scale. *Personality and Social Psychology Bulletin, 27,* 151–161. doi:10.1177/0146167201272002

Romero, G. J., Wyatt, G. E., Loeb, T. B., Carmona, J. V., & Solis, B. (1999). The prevalence and circumstances of child sexual abuse among Latina women. *Hispanic Journal of Behavioral Sciences, 21,* 351–365. doi:10.1177/0739986399213009

Sabina, C., Cuevas, C. A., & Schally, J. L. (2012). Help-seeking in a national sample of victimized Latino women: The influence of victimization types. *Journal of Interpersonal Violence, 27,* 40–61. doi:10.1177/0886260511416460

Saleebey, D. (1996). The strengths perspective in social work practice: Extensions and cautions. *Social Work, 3,* 296–305.

Shaw, J. A., Lewis, J. E., Loeb, A., Rosado, J., & Rodriguez, R. (2001). A comparison of Hispanic and African-American sexually abused girls and their families. *Child Abuse and Neglect, 25,* 1363–1379. doi:10.1016/S0145-2134(01)00272-1

Smith, R. L., & Montilla, R. E. (2015). *Counseling and family therapy with Latino populations: Strategies that work (family therapy and counseling)* (1st ed.). New York: Routledge.

Smokowski, P. R., & Bacallao, M. (2009). Entre dos mundos/ Between two world's youth violence prevention: Comparing psychodramatic and support group delivery formats. *Small Group Research, 40,* 3–27. doi:10.1177/1046496408326771

Srinivas, T., & DePrince, A. P. (2015). Links between the police response and women's psychological outcomes following intimate partner violence. *Violence and Victims, 30,* 32–48. doi:10.1891/0886-6708.VV-D-13-00109

Stover, C., Berkman, M., Desai, R., & Marans, S. (2010). The efficacy of a police-advocacy intervention for victims of domestic violence: 12 month follow-up data. *Violence Against Women, 16,* 410–425. doi:10.1177/1077801210364046

Stover, C. S., Rainey, A. M., Berkman, M. & Marans, S. (2008). Factors associated with engagement in a police-advocacy home-visit intervention to prevent domestic violence. *Violence Against Women, 14,* 1430–1450. doi:1177/1077801208327019

Strozdas, L. J. (2004). Moral evil close to home: Responding to domestic violence. *New Theology Review, 17,* 26–37.

Suarez, E. B. (2013). The association between post-traumatic stress-related symptoms, resilience, current stress and past exposure to violence: A cross sectional study of the survival of Quechua women in the aftermath of the Peruvian armed conflict. *Conflict and Health, 7,* 1–11. doi:10.1186/1752-1505-7-21.

Taylor, N. & Mouzos, J. (2006). *Community attitudes to violence against women survey: A full technical report.* Victoria: Australian Government, Australian Institute of Criminology.

Ting, S. R. (2008). Meta-analysis on dating violence prevention among middle and high schools. *Journal of School Violence, 8,* 328–337. doi:10.1080/15388220903130197

Toseland, R. W., & Rivas, R. F. (2017). *An introduction to group work practice: Connecting core competencies series* (8th ed.). Boston, MA: Pearson Education.

Ulibarri, M. D., Ulloa, E. C., & Camacho, L. (2009). Prevalence of sexually abusive experiences in childhood and adolescence among a community sample of Latinas: A descriptive study. *Journal of Child Sexual Abuse, 18,* 405–421. doi:10.1080/10538710903051088

Ullman, S. E., & Filipas, H. H. (2005). Ethnicity and child sexual abuse experiences of female college students. *Journal of Child Sexual Abuse, 14,* 67–89. doi:10.1300/J070v14n03_04

Ulloa, E. O., Jaycox, L. H., Skinner, S. K., & Orsburn, M. M. (2008). Attitudes about violence and dating among Latino/a boys and girls. *Journal of Ethnic and Cultural Diversity, 17,* 157–176. doi:10.1080/15313200801941721

Umaña-Taylor, A. J., & Fine, M. A. (2003). Predicting commitment to wed among Hispanic and Anglo partners. *Journal of Marriage and Family, 65,* 117–139. doi:10.1111/j.1741-3737.2003.00117.x

Updegraff, K. A., McHale, S. M., & Whiteman, S. D. (2005). Adolescent sibling relationships in Mexican American families: Exploring the role of *familism*. *Journal of Family Psychology, 19*, 512–522. doi:10.1037/0893- 3200.19.4.512

U.S. Census Bureau. (2010a). *Current population survey: Annual social and economic supplement.* Retrieved February 20, 2012, from http://www.census.gov/population/www/socdemo/hispanic/reports.html

U.S. Census Bureau. (2010b). *QuickFacts.* Retrieved from http://www.census.gov/quickfacts/table/PST045215/1780060,00

U.S. Conference of Catholic Bishops. (2002). *When I call for help: A pastoral response to domestic violence against women.* Retrieved July 13, 2010, from http://www.usccb.org/laity/help.htm

U.S. Conference of Catholic Bishops. (2003). *Strangers no longer: Together on the journey of hope.* Retrieved July 13, 2010, from http://www.usccb.org/issues-and-action/human-life-and-dignity/immigration/strangers-no-longer-together-on-the-journey-of-hope.cfm

U.S. Department of Justice. (2015). *Application for cancellation of removal and adjustment of status for certain nonpermanent residents.* Retrieved October 29, 2015, from Executive Office for Immigration Review: http://www.justice.gov/sites/default/files/pages/attachments/2015/07/24/eoir42b.pdf

Vazquez, C., & Rosa, D. (2011). *Grief therapy with Latinos: Integrating culture for clinicians* (1st ed.). New York: Springer.

Vera, M., Alegría, M., Pattatucci-Aragón, A. M., & Peña, M. (2005). Childhood sexual abuse and drug use among low-income urban Puerto Rican women. *Journal of Social Work Practice in the Addictions, 5*, 45–68. doi:10.1300/J160v05n01_03

Vidales, G. T. (2010). Arrested justice: The multifaceted plight of immigrant Latinas who faced domestic violence. *Journal of Family Violence, 25*, 533–544. doi:10.1007/s10896-010-93095

Walker, L. E. (1979). *The battered woman.* New York: Harper & Row.

Walker, L. E. (2002). The politics of trauma practice: Politics, psychology and the battered woman's movement. *Journal of Trauma Practice, 1*, 81–102.

Walker, S. L., & Smith, D. J. (2009). "Children at risk": Development, implementation, and effectiveness of a school-based violence intervention and prevention program. *Journal of Prevention & Intervention in the Community, 37*, 316–325. doi:10.1080/10852350903196316

Watson, B., & Halford, W. K. (2010). Classes of childhood sexual abuse and women's adult couple relationships. *Violence and Victims, 25*, 518–535. doi:10.1007/s10567-010-0066-z

Wendt, S. (2008). Christianity and domestic violence: Feminist poststructuralist perspectives. *Affilia: Journal of Women and Social Work, 23*, 144–155. doi:10.1177/0886109908314326

Weiner, M. H. (2003). The potential and challenges of transnational litigation for feminists concerned about domestic violence here and abroad. *Journal of Gender, Social Policy and the Law, 11*(2), 749–800. Retrieved from http://digitalcommons.wcl.american.edu/jgspl/vol11/iss2/19/

Welland, C., & Ribner, N. (2007). *Healing from violence: Latino men's journey to a new masculinity* (1st ed.). New York: Springer.

Welland, C., & Wexler, D. (2007). *Sin golpes: Cómo transformar la respuesta violenta de los hombres en la pareja y la familia.* Ciudad de México: Editorial Pax Mexico.

Whitaker, D. J., Baker, C. K., Pratt, C., Reed, E., Suri, S., Pavlos, C., Nagy, B. J., & Silverman, J. (2007). A network model for providing culturally competent services for partner violence and sexual violence. *Violence Against Women, 13*, 190–209. doi:10.1177/1077801206296984

Wolff, D. A., Burleigh, D., Tripp, M., & Gadomski, A. (2001). Training clergy: The role of the faith community in domestic violence prevention. *Journal of Religion & Abuse, 2*, 47–60.

Young, C. (2004). Healthy relationships: Where's the research? *The Family Journal: Counseling and Therapy for Couples and Families, 2*, 159–162. doi:10.1177/1066480703262090

Zink, T., Klesges, L., Levin, L., & Putnam, F. (2007). Abuse behavior inventory. *Journal of Interpersonal Violence, 22*, 921–931. doi:10.1177/0886260507301228

Zust, B. L. (2006). Meaning of INSIGHT participation among women who have experienced intimate partner violence. *Issues in Mental Health Nursing, 27*,, 775–793. doi:10.1080/01612840600781170

APPENDIX A

Sample of Resources in the State of Minnesota

MENTAL HEALTH AND DOMESTIC VIOLENCE RESOURCES

Domestic Violence Hotlines Day One Minnesota Domestic Violence Crisis Line: 1 (866) 223-1111

National Domestic Violence Hotline: 1 (800) 799-SAFE (7233) www.thehotline.org

Agency	City	Crisis Business Phone	Services	Spanish-Speaking Services
African American Family Services www.aafs.net	Minneapolis	(612) 871-7878	Focus on black community; advocacy; family counseling	
Alexandra House http://www.alexandrahouse.org/pages.php	Blaine and Anoka	(612) 780-2330 (612) 780-2332	Free services including emergency shelter, legal and hospital-based advocacy, support, a 24-hour crisis line, economic assistance, safety planning, housing resources, support, community education, training, youth violence prevention, and information groups	Spanish-speaking staff and volunteers. Interpreters provided when needed
Asian Women United of America www.awum.org	St. Paul	(612) 724-8823 (612) 724-0756	Services for women victims of DV; Hmong-, Cambodian-, Vietnamese-, Hindu-, and Japanese-speaking advocates; court advocacy; help with orders for protection	No Spanish-speaking services
Aurora Center for Advocacy and Education www.umn.edu/aurora	Minneapolis	(612) 626-9111 (612) 626-2929	Free and confidential advocacy; referral services regarding sexual assault, relationship violence, and stalking for students, staff, and faculty of the University of Minnesota; legal advocacy involving harassment restraining orders and orders for protection	Several advocates who speak Spanish
Battered Women's Legal Advocacy Project http://www.bwlap.org/dvic	St. Paul	1 (800) 313-2666 (612) 343-9842	Legal advocacy, support, legal representation, and outreach for immigrant women and children. training, technical assistance, and advocacy for issues of stalking; formulating proactive protocols for DV agencies	Spanish-speaking services
Casa de Esperanza www.casadeesperanza.org	St. Paul	(651) 772-1611 (651) 646-5553	Shelter; advocacy; education; referrals for Hispanic women and children; leadership development program for Latinas	All staff speak Spanish and English. Bilingual crisis line

Organization	City	Phone	Services	Language Services
Children's Home Society and Family Services www.chsfs.org	St. Paul and Roseville	(952) 432-4145	Groups for women and men in violent relationships; individual counseling for children; domestic abuse and anger management services for teens	No Spanish interpreter
Chrysalis www.chyrsaliswomen.org	Minneapolis	(612) 870-2426	Individual, group, family, and couples counseling	No Spanish-speaking counselors
Civil Society www.civilsociety.org	St. Paul	(651) 291-0713	Legal services: court advocacy/accompaniment;Minnesota Crime Victims Reparation Board (assistance with application); crisis and short-term individual, family, and group counseling; community education and training; assistance with legal protection orders	Spanish services available
CLUES (Chicano-Latino United in Service) www.clues.org	St. Paul	(651) 379-4200	Mental health, chemical health, and sexual assault bicultural counseling for Hispanics; parent education, case management, and fatherhood programs; economic advancement services; community health worker services	Bicultural counseling for Hispanics. Spanish-speaking services
Community University Health Care Center http://www.cuhcc.umn.edu/home.html	Minneapolis	(612) 627-4774	Free and confidential advocacy services for victims of DV and sexual assault	Spanish-speaking staff
Women's Advocates http://www.wadvocates.org/	St. Paul	(651) 227-8284 (651) 227-9966	Shelter, advocacy, mental health therapy, aftercare services for women and children	Interpreters available
Cornerstone Advocacy Services http://www.cornerstonemn.org/index.php	Bloomington	(952) 884-0330 (952) 884-0376	Emergency safe housing for adults and children, advocacy, support, individual counseling for DV victims and violent youth, shelter for men, emergency shelter for women and children, protection for pets, school-based violence prevention, legal services, transitional and permanent housing program, support groups, parenting skills, life skills, senior women's advocacy, stalking response	

(Continued)

Domestic Violence Hotlines — Day One Minnesota Domestic Violence Crisis Line: 1 (866) 223-1111

National Domestic Violence Hotline: 1 (800) 799-SAFE (7233) www.thehotline.org

Agency	City	Crisis Business Phone	Services	Spanish-Speaking Services
Communication Service for the Deaf (CSD) of Minnesota Deaf Domestic Violence Program www.csd.org	St. Paul	(651) 487-8867 dvhelp@skytel.com (crisis email/pager)	Shelter and safe housing, advocacy, for deaf victims	
Community-University Health Care Center (CUHCC) www.ahc.umn.edu/cuhcc/	Minneapolis	(612) 638-0700	Culturally sensitive, free, and confidential advocacy services with bilingual workers; legal clinic	Spanish-speaking staff. For Spanish interpreter call (612) 638-0746
Domestic Abuse Project http://www. domesticabuseproject.com/ about-dap/	Minneapolis	Women: (612) 673-3526 Men: (612) 874-7063	Shelter, clothing, lock changes, for victims of DV. Therapy for women who are victims of DV, for men who use abuse in intimate relationships, for children who witness DV, and adolescents who use abuse in dating relationships	Spanish-speaking legal and community advocate serving Minneapolis (and other areas if needed). Group (called *Hombria*) for Spanish-speaking men who have used abusive behavior meets Thursday evenings
Eastside Neighborhood Service http://www.esns.org/ FamilyViolence	Minneapolis	(612) 787-4056	Programs for men and women who struggle with anger and assaultive behavior	

Organization	Location	Phone	Services	Spanish Services
ESS Emergency Social Services www.redcrossmn.org	St. Paul	(651) 291-6795	After 5 PM and weekends; shelter, transport for abuse victims	Spanish interpreters
Face to Face www.face2face.org	St. Paul	(651) 772-5555	Adolescent incest and sexual assault victims support groups; individual counseling; prenatal and medical clinic	
Family & Children's Services www.thefamilypartnership.org	Minneapolis	English: (612) 728-2061 Spanish: (612) 728-2089	SAFE families program: Provides safety planning and support for survivors, planning and intervention for batterers, resources, referrals, support network, training on violence and intervention. Services are free	All services are offered in Spanish and English
Tubman Family Alliance www.harriettubman.org www.StopFamilyViolence.org	Minneapolis	(612) 825-0000 (West Metro) (651) 770-0777 (East Metro) (612) 825-3333	Criminal and civil court legal advocacy; transitional services; crisis services and shelters for women; crisis services for men; youth and family services; prevention and community involvement programs; counseling services for abusers; fathering classes; support groups; serves Ramsey County, Washington County, and Hennepin County	Spanish-speaking legal advocates. Spanish translators at shelters. No mental health services in Spanish at this time
Hispanos en Minnesota www.hispanosenminnesota.org	Statewide	(651) 227-0831	Support groups for Hispanic women; DWI clinic; chemical dependency education	Spanish support groups and services
Hennepin County Legal Advocacy Project	Minneapolis	(612) 348-4003	Domestic violence shelters, counseling, groups, and support	Spanish-speaking advocates/attorneys
Home Free Shelter http://www.missionsinc.org/programs/home-free	Plymouth	(612) 559-4945 (612) 559-9008	Emergency housing, advocacy, transportation, legal advocacy, education, childcare, and support services for women and children. Serving women in Northwest Hennepin County and other municipalities	Spanish-speaking advocates
360 Communities Food Shelf and Lewis House http://360communities.org/services/lewis_house.aspx	Eagan and Hastings	(952) 985-5300 (651) 452-7288 (Eagan) (651) 437-1291 (Hastings)	Food shelf, safe housing, support and advocacy to survivors of domestic abuse and sexual assault; prevention, education, and outreach services	Spanish-speaking volunteers and interns at both shelters

(Continued)

| Domestic Violence Hotlines | Day One Minnesota Domestic Violence Crisis Line: 1 (866) 223-1111 | | | |
| | National Domestic Violence Hotline: 1 (800) 799-SAFE (7233) www.thehotline.org | | | |

Agency	City	Crisis Business Phone	Services	Spanish-Speaking Services
Men's Center www.tcmc.org	Minneapolis	(612) 822-5892	Daily support groups and workshops for men	
Minnesota Resources for Fathers http://www.resourcesforfathers.org/resources.html	Minneapolis, St. Paul, Blaine	(763) 783-4938	Phone counseling and referrals for men to find an alternative to violence; DV courses and aftercare	
North Memorial Medical Women's Center	Robbinsdale	(763) 520-7070 (763) 520-2639	DV support programs	Access to interpreters. Referrals to Spanish-speaking resources
Outfront Minnesota www.outfront.org	Minneapolis	(612) 824-8424 (612) 822-0127, ext. 7656	Advocacy; support; counseling; safe house referrals for LGBT victims of domestic abuse and harassment; referral services for people with abusive behavior	
Project PEACE www.projectpeace.org	Brooklyn Center	(612) 536-1850 (763) 533-0733	Advocacy; crisis intervention; safety planning; legal advocates; educational support groups. Serving Brooklyn Center, Maple Grove, Crytsal, and Robbinsdale	No Spanish-speaking advocates

Organization	Location	Phone	Services	Language Services
Sexual Offense Services (SOS) www.co.ramsey.mn.us/ph/yas/sos.htm	St. Paul	(651) 643-3006 (651) 643-3022	No charge; referrals; counseling; support groups for both male and female victims of sexual assault; support groups for parents of victims. Monday nights open support group 6–9:30 PM	Interpretation services offered through language line, male or female, three-way conversation. Counseling and support groups are in English
Sojourner	Hopkins	(612) 933-7422 (952) 935-1004	Advocacy for victims of DV, emergency shelter	Interpreters available if needed
Southern Minnesota Regional Legal Services www.smrls.org	St. Paul	(651) 224-1775 (651) 222-5863(TDD)	Legal assistance for low-income victims of domestic abuse in civil and family court	Spanish-speaking advocates available
Southern Valley Intervention Project	Chaska	(952) 873-4214 (612) 448-4489	Advocacy; shelters; emergency assistance; support groups; criminal intervention advocates	General advocacy and criminal and legal advocacy provided in Spanish
St. Paul Intervention Project www.stpaulintervention.org	St. Paul	(651) 645-2824 (612) 645-2824	Information; referrals; support groups; legal advocacy in criminal and civil court matters; includes Hmong and Spanish advocates	Spanish-speaking advocates
Womankind	Edina	(952) 924-5775	Support services for battered women	
Women of Nations http://www.women-of-nations.org/Contact_Us.html	St. Paul	(651) 222-5836 (877) 209-1266 651) 251-1603	Provides culturally competent services for all women; culturally specific services for Native American women; shelter; community and legal advocates; referrals	Interpreters and referral to Spanish-speaking services

Note. DV = domestic violence; LGBT = lesbian, gay, bisexual, and transgender.

APPENDIX B

NATIONAL WEBSITES AND PHONE NUMBERS ON DOMESTIC VIOLENCE

National Domestic Violence Hotline:
1 (800) 799-SAFE (7233)
http://www.thehotline.org/

Domestic Violence Resource Center
24-hour crisis line: toll free at 1 (866) 469-8600 or (503) 469-8620
http://www.dvrc-or.org/

Casa de Esperanza: National Latin@ Network of Healthy Families and Communities
Bilingual national hotline: (651) 772-1611
http://www.casadeesperanza.org/

Safe Horizon
Crisis hotline: 1 (800) 621-HOPE (4673)
http://www.safehorizon.org/

Rape, Abuse and Incest National Network
Crisis hotline: 1 (800) 656-HOPE (4673)
https://rainn.org/

National Resource Center on Domestic Violence
http://www.nrcdv.org/

National Network to End Domestic Violence
http://nnedv.org/

National Coalition Against Domestic Violence
http://www.ncadv.org/
https://www.domesticshelters.org/ (national domestic violence shelters)

National Health Resource Center on Domestic Violence
http://www.futureswithoutviolence.org/health/national-health-resource-center-on-domestic-violence/

TEEN DATING WHEEL

EQUALITY WHEEL FOR TEENS

NONVIOLENCE

NEGOTIATION AND FAIRNESS:
Seeking mutually satisfying resolutions to conflict. Accepting changes. Being willing to compromise.

NON-THREATENING BEHAVIOR:
Talking and acting so that she feels safe and comfortable expressing herself and doing things.

COMMUNICATION:
Willingness to have open and spontaneous dialogue. Having a balance of giving and receiving. Problem solving to mutual benefit. Learning to compromise without one overshadowing the other.

RESPECT:
Listening to her non-judgmentally. Being emotionally affirming and understanding. Valuing her opinions.

TEEN EQUALITY

SHARED POWER:
Taking mutual responsibility for recognizing influence on the relationship. Making decisions together.

TRUST AND SUPPORT:
Supporting her goals in life. Respecting her right to her own feelings, friends, activities, and opinions.

SELF-CONFIDENCE AND PERSONAL GROWTH:
Respecting her personal identity and encouraging her individual growth and freedom. Supporting her security in her own worth.

HONESTY AND ACCOUNTABILITY:
Accepting responsibility for self. Acknowledging past use of violence. Admitting being wrong. Communicating openly and truthfully.

NONVIOLENCE

RUEDA DE IGUALDADE PARA LOS JOVENES

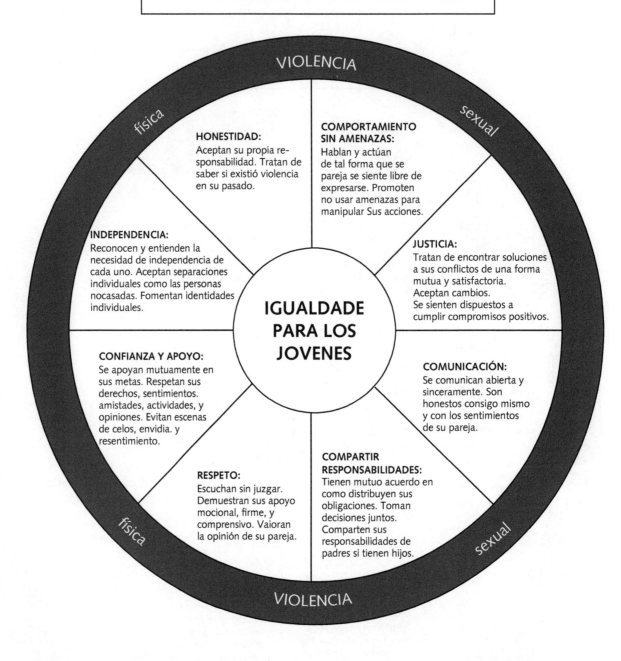

VIOLENCIA

física

sexual

HONESTIDAD:
Aceptan su propia responsabilidad. Tratan de saber si existió violencia en su pasado.

COMPORTAMIENTO SIN AMENAZAS:
Hablan y actúan de tal forma que se pareja se siente libre de expresarse. Promoten no usar amenazas para manipular Sus acciones.

INDEPENDENCIA:
Reconocen y entienden la necesidad de independencia de cada uno. Aceptan separaciones individuales como las personas nocasadas. Fomentan identidades individuales.

JUSTICIA:
Tratan de encontrar soluciones a sus conflictos de una forma mutua y satisfactoria. Aceptan cambios. Se sienten dispuestos a cumplir compromisos positivos.

IGUALDADE PARA LOS JOVENES

CONFIANZA Y APOYO:
Se apoyan mutuamente en sus metas. Respetan sus derechos, sentimientos. amistades, actividades, y opiniones. Evitan escenas de celos, envidia. y resentimiento.

COMUNICACIÓN:
Se comunican abierta y sinceramente. Son honestos consigo mismo y con los sentimientos de su pareja.

RESPETO:
Escuchan sin juzgar. Demuestran sus apoyo mocional, firme, y comprensivo. Vaioran la opinión de su pareja.

COMPARTIR RESPONSABILIDADES:
Tienen mutuo acuerdo en como distribuyen sus obligaciones. Toman decisiones juntos. Comparten sus responsabilidades de padres si tienen hijos.

física

sexual

VIOLENCIA

TEEN POWER AND CONTROL WHEEL

VIOLENCE

physical

sexual

PEER PRESSURE:
Threatening to expose someone's weakness or spread rumors. Telling malicious lies about an individual to peer group.

ANGER/EMOTIONAL ABUSE:
Putting her/him down. Making her/him feel bad about her or himself. Name calling. Making her/him think she/he's crazy. Playing mind games. Humiliating one another. Making her/him feel guilty

ISOLATION/EXCLUSION:
Controlling what another does, who she/he sees and talks to, what she/he reads, where she/he goes. Limiting outside involvement. Using jealousy to justify actions

USING SOCIAL STATUS:
Treating her like a servant. Making all the decisions. Acting like the "master of the castle." Being the one to define men's and women's roles.

TEEN POWER AND CONTROL

SEXUAL COERCION:
Manipulating or making threats to get sex. Getting her pregnant. Threatening to take the children away. Getting someone drunk or drugged to get sex.

INTIMIDATION:
Making someone afraid by using looks, actions, gestures. Smashing things. Destroying property. Abusing pets. Displaying weapons.

THREATS:
Making and/or carrying out threats to do something to hurt another. Threatening to leave, to commit suicide, to report her/him to the police. Making her/him drop charges. Making her/him do illegal things.

MINIMIZE/DENY/ BLAME:
Making light of the abuse and not taking concerns about it seriously. Saying the abuse didn't happen. Shifting responsibility for abusive behavior. Saying she/he caused it.

physical

sexual

VIOLENCE

Poder y Control en el Noviazgo

Cuando una persona en una relación repetidamente asusta o le hace daño a la otra persona es abuso. La rueda de poder y control nombra ejemplos de cada forma de abuso. Acuérdense que abuso es mucho más que pegar o agarrar a alguien.

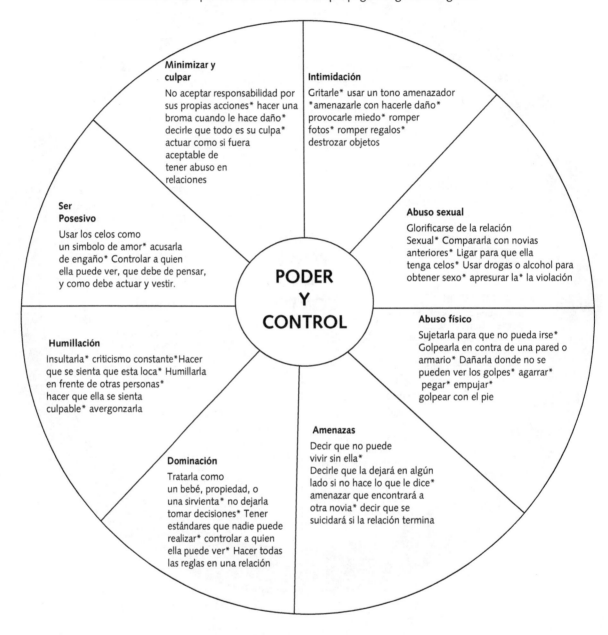

Minimizar y culpar

No aceptar responsabilidad por sus propias acciones* hacer una broma cuando le hace daño* decirle que todo es su culpa* actuar como si fuera aceptable de tener abuso en relaciones

Intimidación

Gritarle* usar un tono amenazador *amenazarle con hacerle daño* provocarle miedo* romper fotos* romper regalos* destrozar objetos

Ser Posesivo

Usar los celos como un simbolo de amor* acusarla de engaño* Controlar a quien ella puede ver, que debe de pensar, y como debe actuar y vestir.

Abuso sexual

Glorificarse de la relación Sexual* Compararla con novias anteriores* Ligar para que ella tenga celos* Usar drogas o alcohol para obtener sexo* apresurar la* la violación

Humillación

Insultarla* criticismo constante*Hacer que se sienta que esta loca* Humillarla en frente de otras personas* hacer que ella se sienta culpable* avergonzarla

Abuso físico

Sujetarla para que no pueda irse* Golpearla en contra de una pared o armario* Dañarla donde no se pueden ver los golpes* agarrar* pegar* empujar* golpear con el pie

Dominación

Tratarla como un bebé, propiedad, o una sirvienta* no dejarla tomar decisiones* Tener estándares que nadie puede realizar* controlar a quien ella puede ver* Hacer todas las reglas en una relación

Amenazas

Decir que no puede vivir sin ella* Decirle que la dejará en algún lado si no hace lo que le dice* amenazar que encontrará a otra novia* decir que se suicidará si la relación termina

PODER Y CONTROL

CHARACTERISTICS OF HEALTHY RELATIONSHIPS

How many of the following attitudes and behaviors are present in your relationship?

- ☐ communication is open and spontaneous (including listening)
- ☐ rules/boundaries are clear and explicit yet allow flexibility
- ☐ individuality, freedom, and personal identity are enhanced
- ☐ each enjoys doing things for self, as well as for the other
- ☐ play, humor, and having fun together is commonplace
- ☐ each does not attempt to "fix" or control the other
- ☐ acceptance of self and other (for real selves)
- ☐ assertiveness: feelings and needs are expressed
- ☐ humility: able to let go of need to "be right"
- ☐ self-confidence and security in own worth
- ☐ conflict is faced directly and resolved
- ☐ openness to constructive feedback
- ☐ each is trustful of the other
- ☐ balance of giving and receiving
- ☐ negotiations are fair and democratic
- ☐ tolerance: forgiveness of self and other
- ☐ mistakes are accepted and learned from
- ☐ willingness to take risks and be vulnerable
- ☐ other meaningful relationships and interests exist
- ☐ each can enjoy being alone and privacy is respected
- ☐ personal growth, change, and exploration are encouraged
- ☐ continuity and consistency are present in the commitment
- ☐ good balance of oneness (closeness) and separation from each other
- ☐ responsibility for own behaviors and happiness (not blaming other)

Remember, developing healthy relationships is an important life skill.

Note: The author of this handout is unknown. The handout was obtained at a domestic violence training.

Características de las Relaciones Saludables
¿Cuántas de las siguientes actitudes y comportamientos están presentes en su relación?

- [ ] comunicación es abierta y espontánea (incluyendo el escuchar)
- [ ] reglas/límites son claros y explícitos, sin embargo, permite la flexibilidad
- [ ] individualidad, la libertad y la identidad personal se ve reforzada
- [ ] cada disfruta de hacer las cosas por uno mismo, así como para el otro
- [ ] juego, el humor, y se divierten juntos
- [ ] cada no intenta "corregir" o controlar a la otra
- [ ] aceptación del yo y el otro (para ser real)
- [ ] asertividad: los sentimientos y las necesidades se expresan
- [ ] humildad: capaz de dejar de lado la necesidad de "tener razón"
- [ ] auto- confianza
- [ ] conflicto se enfrenta directamente y se resolvió
- [ ] apertura a la crítica constructiva
- [ ] cada uno es de confianza de la otra
- [ ] equilibrio de dar y recibir
- [ ] negociaciones sean justas y democráticas
- [ ] tolerancia: el perdón de uno mismo y los demás
- [ ] errores son aceptados y aprendieron de ellos
- [ ] disposición a tomar riesgos y ser vulnerables
- [ ] existen otras relaciones e intereses significativos
- [ ] cada uno puede disfrutar de estar solo y se respeta la privacidad
- [ ] se fomenta el crecimiento personal, el cambio y la exploración
- [ ] continuidad y consistencia está presente en el compromiso
- [ ] equilibrio de la unidad (cercanía) y la separación entre sí
- [ ] la responsabilidad de su propio comportamiento y la felicidad (no culpar a otro)

Recuerde, el desarrollo de relaciones sanas es una importante habilidad para la vida.
Nota: Autor del material es desconocido. Folleto fue obtenida en una formación de violencia doméstica.

EQUALITY WHEEL

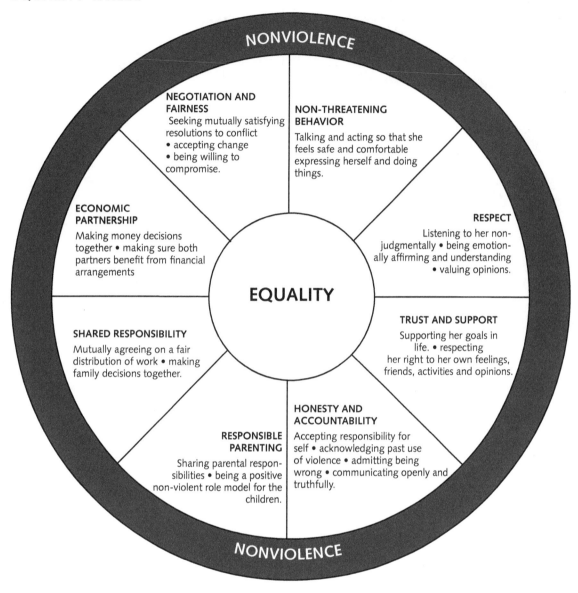

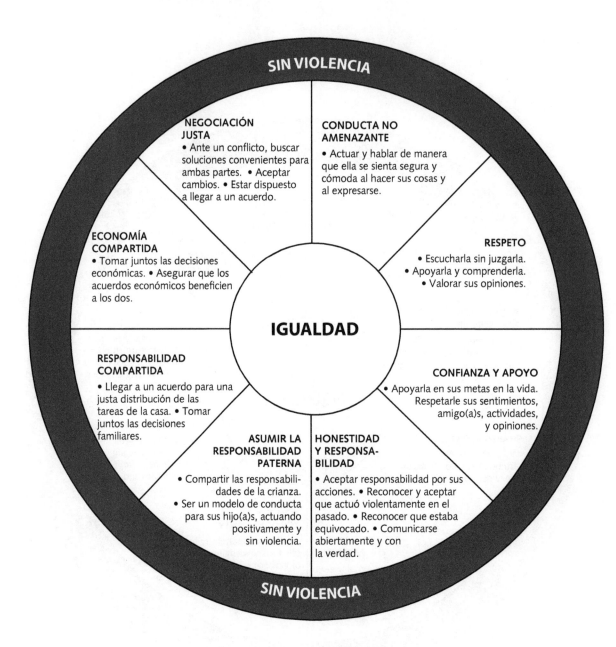

SIN VIOLENCIA

NEGOCIACIÓN JUSTA
• Ante un conflicto, buscar soluciones convenientes para ambas partes. • Aceptar cambios. • Estar dispuesto a llegar a un acuerdo.

CONDUCTA NO AMENAZANTE
• Actuar y hablar de manera que ella se sienta segura y cómoda al hacer sus cosas y al expresarse.

ECONOMÍA COMPARTIDA
• Tomar juntos las decisiones económicas. • Asegurar que los acuerdos económicos beneficien a los dos.

RESPETO
• Escucharla sin juzgarla. • Apoyarla y comprenderla. • Valorar sus opiniones.

IGUALDAD

RESPONSABILIDAD COMPARTIDA
• Llegar a un acuerdo para una justa distribución de las tareas de la casa. • Tomar juntos las decisiones familiares.

CONFIANZA Y APOYO
• Apoyarla en sus metas en la vida. Respetarle sus sentimientos, amigo(a)s, actividades, y opiniones.

ASUMIR LA RESPONSABILIDAD PATERNA
• Compartir las responsabilidades de la crianza. • Ser un modelo de conducta para sus hijo(a)s, actuando positivamente y sin violencia.

HONESTIDAD Y RESPONSABILIDAD
• Aceptar responsabilidad por sus acciones. • Reconocer y aceptar que actuó violentamente en el pasado. • Reconocer que estaba equivocado. • Comunicarse abiertamente y con la verdad.

SIN VIOLENCIA

POWER AND CONTROL WHEEL

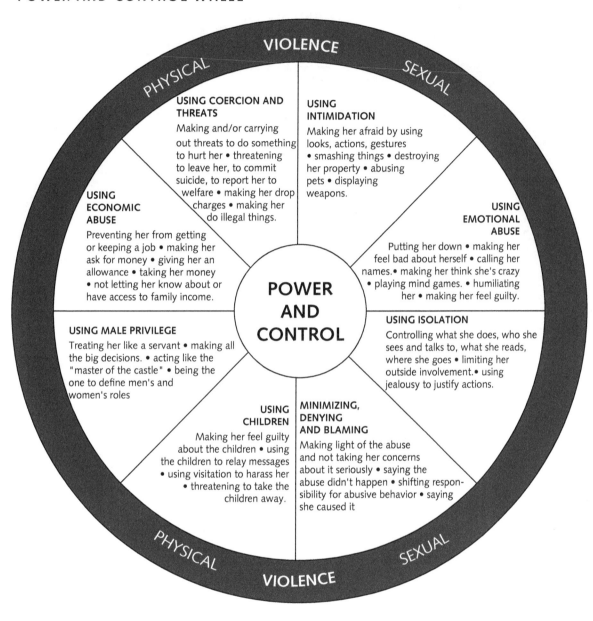

VIOLENCIA

FÍSICA

SEXUAL

USO DE COERCIÓN Y AMENAZAS
• Asustarla con amenazas de hacerle mal.
• Amenazarla con dejarla, con el suicidio o con denunciarla falsamente a la autoridad.
• Obligarla a retirar los cargos presentados contra él
• Obligarla a cometer actos ilegales.

INTIMIDACIÓN
• Provocarle miedo a través de sus miradas, acciones y gestos. • Destrozar objetos.
• Intimidarla rompiéndole sus cosas personales, maltratando a los animales domésticos, mostrándole armas.

ABUSO ECONÓMICO
• No dejarla trabajar o impedirle que mantenga su empleo. • Obligarla a que le pida dinero. • Darle una mensualidad. • Quitarle el dinero.
• No informarle acerca de los ingresos familiares o no permitirle disponer de los ingresos.

ABUSO EMOCIONAL
• Hacerla sentir inferior.
• Hacerla sentir mal. • Insultarla con apodos ofensivos. Hacerla pensar que está loca.
• Confundirla a propósito.
• Humillarla. • Hacerla sentir culpable.

PODER Y CONTROL

PRIVILEGIO MASCULINO
• Tratarla como una sirvienta
• No dejarla tomar decisiones importantes.
• Actuar como el rey de la casa.
• Definir los roles del hombre y de la mujer.

AISLAMIENTO
• Controlar lo que hace, a quién puede ver, con quién puede hablar, lo que puede leer, y dónde va. • Limitarle su vida social. Utilizar los celos para justificar sus actos.

MANIPULACIÓN DE LOS NIÑO(A)S
• Hacerla sentir culpable por el comportamiento de los niño(a)s. • Usar a los niño(a)s como intermediarios y mantener así el control. • Usar las visitas con los niño(a)s para molestarla o amenazarla. • Amenazarla con quitarle los niño(a)s.

MINIMIZAR, NEGAR, CULPAR
• Minimizar el abuso.
• No tomar seriamente la preocupación que ella tiene sobre el abuso. • Negar que hubo abuso.
• Hacerla sentir responsable de la conducta abusiva.
• Decirle que ella lo provocó.

FÍSICA

SEXUAL

VIOLENCIA

- -

APPENDIX G

SAFETY PLANNING WORKSHEET

Domestic Violence Personalized Safety Plan

Name: _____ Date: _____

The following steps represent my plan for increasing my safety and preparing in advance for the possibility of further violence. Although I d not have control over my partner's violence, I do have a choice about how to respond to him/her and how to best get myself and my children to safety.

STEP 1: Safety during a violence incident. *Women cannot always avoid violent incidents. To increase safety, battered women may use a variety of strategies.*

I can use some of the following strategies:

A. If I decide to leave, I will _____.
   (Practice how to get out safely. What door, windows, elevators, stairwells, or fire escapes would you use?)

B. I can keep my purse and car keys ready and put them *(location)* _____ to leave quickly.

C. I can tell _____ about the violence and request that he or she call the police if he or she hears suspicious noises coming from my house.

D. I can teach my children how to use the telephone to contact the police, the fire department, and 911.

E. I will use _____ as my code with my children or my friends so they can call for help.

F. If I have to leave my home, I will go to _____.
   (Decide this even if you don't think there will be a next time.)

G. I can also teach some of these strategies to some or all of my children.

H. When I expect we're going to have an argument, I'll try to move to a place that is low risk, such as _____. *(Try to avoid arguments in the bathroom, garage, kitchen, near weapons, or in rooms without access to an outside door.)*

I. I will use my judgment and intuition. If the situation is very serious, I can give my partner what he or she wants to calm him or her down. I have to protect myself until I/we are out of danger.

STEP 2: Safety when preparing to leave. *Battered women frequently leave the residence they share with the battering partner. Leaving must be done with a careful plan to increase safety. Batterers often strike back when they believe that a battered woman is leaving a relationship.*

I can use some or all of the following strategies:

A. I will leave money and an extra set of keys with _____ so I can leave quickly.

B. I will keep copies of important documents or keys at _____.

C. I will open a savings account by _____, to increase my independence.

D. Other things I can do to increase my independence, include: _____
   _____.

E. I can keep change for phone calls on me at all times. I understand that if I use my telephone credit card, the following month's phone bill will show my batterer those numbers I called after I left. To keep my phone communications confidential, I must either use coins, or I might ask to use a friend's phone card for a limited time when I first leave.

F. I will check with _____ and _____ to see who would be able to let me say with them or lend me some money.

G. I can leave extra clothes or money with _____.

H. I will sit down and review my safety plan every _____ to plan the safest way to leave the residence. _____ *(domestic violence advocate or friend's name)* has agreed to help me review this plan.

I. I will rehearse my escape plan and, as appropriate, practice it with my children.

STEP 3: Safety in my own residence. *There are many things that a woman can do to increase her safety in her own residence. It may be impossible to do everything at once, but safety measures can be added step by step.*

Safety measures I can use:

A. I can change the locks on my doors and windows as soon as possible.

B. I can replace wooden doors with steel/metal doors.

C. I can install security systems, including additional locks, window bars, poles to wedge against doors, an electronic system, etc.

D. I can purchase rope ladders to be used for escape from second-floor windows.

E. I can install smoke detectors and fire extinguishers on each floor of my house/apartment.

F. I can install an outside lighting system that activates when a person is close to the house.

G. I will teach my children how to make a collect call to me and to _____ *(name of friend, etc.)* in the event that my partner takes the children.

H. I will tell the people who take care of my children which people have permission to pick up my children and that partner is not permitted to do so. The people I will inform about pick-up permission include:

_____ *(name of school)*

_____ *(name of babysitter)*

_____ *(name of teacher)*

_____ *(name of Sunday-school teacher)*

_____ *(name[s] of others)*

I. I can inform _____ *(neighbor)* and _____ *(friend)* that my partner no longer resides with me and that they should call law enforcement if he/she is observed near my residence.

STEP 4: Safety with an order of protection. *Many batterers obey protection orders, but one can never be sure which the violent partner will obey and which will violate protective orders. I recognize that I may need to ask law enforcement and the courts to enforce my protective order.*

The following are some steps I can take to help the enforcement of my protection order:

A. I will keep my protection order _____ *(location). Always keep it on or near your person. If you change purses, that's the first thing that should go into the new purse.*

B. I will give my protection order to law enforcement departments in the community where I work, in those communities where I visit friends or family, and in the community where I live.

C. *There should be county and state registries of protection orders that all law enforcement departments can call to confirm a protection order.* I can check to make sure that my order is on the registry. The telephone numbers for the county and state registries of protection orders are: _____ (county) and _____ (state).

D. I will inform my employer; my minister, rabbi, etc.; my closest friend; and _____ that I have a protection order in effect.

E. If my partner destroys my protection order, I can get another copy from the clerk's office.

F. If law enforcement does not help, I can contact an advocate or an attorney and file a complaint with the chief of police department of the sheriff.

G. If my partner violates the protection order, I can call 911 or law enforcement and report the violation.

STEP 5: Safety on the job and in public. *Each battered woman must decide if and when she will tell others that her partner has battered her and that she may be at continued risk. Friends, family, and coworkers can help to protect women. Each woman should carefully consider which people to invite to help secure her safely.*

I might do any or all of the following:

A. I can inform my boss, the security supervisor, and _____ at work.

B. I can ask _____ to help screen my telephone calls at work.

C. When leaving work, I can _____.

D. If I have a problem while driving home, I can _____.

E. If I use public transit, I can _____.

F. I will go to different grocery stores and shopping malls to conduct my business and shop at hours that are different from those I kept when residing with my battering partner.

G. I can use a different bank and go at hours that are different from those I kept when residing with my battering partner.

STEP 6: Safety and drug or alcohol use. *Most people in this culture use alcohol. Many use mood-altering drugs. Much of this is legal, although some is not. The legal outcomes of using illegal drugs can be very hard on battered women, may hurt their relationships with their children, and can put them at a disadvantage in other legal actions with battering partners. Therefore, women should carefully consider the potential cost of using illegal drugs. Beyond this, the use of alcohol or other drugs can reduce a woman's awareness and ability to act quickly to protect herself from her battering partner. Furthermore, the use of alcohol or other drugs by the batterer may give him or her an excuse to use violence. Specific safety plans must be made concerning drugs or alcohol use.*

If drug or alcohol use has occurred in my relationship with my battering partner, I can enhance my safety by doing some or all of the following:

A. If I am going to use, I can do so in a safe place and with people who understand the risk of violence and are committed to my safety.

B. If my partner is using, I can _____ and/or _____.

C. To safeguard my children I might _____.

STEP 7: Safety and my emotional health. *The experience of being battered and verbally degraded by partners is usually exhausting and emotionally draining. The process of building a new life takes much courage and incredible energy.*

To conserve my emotional energy and resources and to avoid hard emotional times, I can do some of the following:

A. If I feel down and am returning to a potentially abusive situation, I can _____ _____.

B. When I have to communicate with my partner in person or by telephone, I can _____ _____.

C. I will try to use "I can . . ." statements with myself and be assertive with others.

D. I can tell myself, "_____" whenever I feel others are trying to control or abuse me.

E. I can read _____ to help me feel stronger.

F. I can call _____ and _____ for support.

G. I can attend workshops and support groups at the domestic violence program or _____ _____ to gain support and strengthen relationships.

STEP 8: Items to take when leaving. *When women leave battering partners it is important to take certain items. Beyond this, women sometimes give an extra copy of papers and an extra set of clothing to a friend just in case they have to leave quickly.*

Money: Even if I never worked, I can take money from jointly held savings and checking accounts. If I do not take this money, my partner can legally take the money and close the accounts.

Items on the following lists with asterisks (*) are the most important to take. If there is time, the other items might be taken, or stored outside the home. These items might best be placed in one location, so that if we have to leave in a hurry, I can grab them quickly. When I leave, I should take:

* Identification for myself
* My birth certificate
* School and vaccination records
* Checkbook, ATM card
* Keys—house, car, office
* Medications
* Welfare identification, work permits, green cards
* Children's birth certificates
* Social Security cards
* Money
* Credit cards
* Driver's license and registration
* Copy of protection order

Passport(s), divorce papers
Medical records—for all family members
Lease/rental agreement, house deed, mortgage payment book
Bank books, insurance papers
Address book
Pictures, jewelry
Children's favorite toys and/or blankets
Items of special sentimental value

Telephone numbers I need to know:
Police/sheriff's department (local)—911 or _____
Police/sheriff's department (work) _____
Police/sheriff's department (school) _____
Prosecutor's office _____
Battered women's program (local) _____
National Domestic Violence Hotline: 1 (800) 799-SAFE (7233) or 1 (800) 787-3224 (TTY) www.thehotline.org
County registry of protection orders _____
State registry of protection orders _____
Work number _____
Supervisor's home number _____

I will keep this document in a safe place and out of reach of my potential attacker.

Review date: _____

Note: Produced and distributed by the National Center on Domestic and Sexual Violence. (2013). Retrieved from http://www.ncdsv.org/publications_safetyplans.html

NATIONAL CENTER
on Domestic and Sexual Violence
training · consulting · advocacy
Tel: 512.407.9020 (voice and fax) · www.ncdsv.org

APPENDIX G

Plan de Seguridad Ante La Violencia Domestica
Se siente segura/o en su hogar? Usted puede hacerlo.
Télefono nacional: 1 (800) 799-SAFE (7233)

Seguridad en el hogar
Seguridad en el trabajo
Protegiendo a sus niños
Consiguiendo una orden de protección

1. Seguridad en el hogar

    Cuando el/la abusador/a esté en el hogar
    -   Manténgase fuera de cuartos sin salida.
    -   Evite los cuartos donde podría haber armas.
    -   Escoja una palabra clave que alerte a sus amistades y hijos para que llamen a la policía.
    -   Deje una maleta y una lista de artículos necesarios en casa de una amistad.

    Cuando el/la abusador/a se haya mudado fuera del hogar
    -   Obtenga una orden de protección.
    -   Cambie las cerraduras en las puertas y ventanas.
    -   Instale una mirilla en la puerta.
    -   Cambie de número de teléfono, verifique quién llama antes de contestar y bloquee las llamadas con un identificador de llamadas "caller ID."
    -   Instale/aumente el alumbrado exterior.
    -   Considere la adquisición de un perro.
    -   Hable con su arrendador o con un vecino acerca de la situación y pídales que llame a la policía si ve en los alrededores al/la abusador/a.

2. Seguridad en el trabajo

    Qué hacer
    -   Hable con su empleador sobre el problema.
    -   Proporcione al departmento de seguridad una fotografía del/de la abusador/a y una copia de la orden de protección.
    -   Verifique quién llama antes de contestar los teléfonos.
    -   Pida que le escolten a su automóvil o al camión.
    -   Cambie de rutas para llegar a su casa.
    -   Considere la adquisición de un teléfono celular para su automóvil.
    -   Lleve con usted una alarma personal o algo que haga ruido.

3. Protegiendo a sus niños
    -   Planee y practique una ruta de escape con sus niños.
    -   Si es seguro, enséñeles una palabra clave para llamar al 911, y cómo utilizar un teléfono público.
    -   Infórmele al personal de la escuela quiénes tienen permiso para recoger a sus niños.
    -   Proporcione al personal de la escuela una fotografía del/de la abusador/a.
    -   Alerte al personal de la escuela que no divulguen a nadie su domicilio ni teléfono.
    -   Consiguiendo una orden de protección
    -   Llame a la agencia legal en su comunidad para informarse sobre una orden de protección y el mandato judicial contra hostigamiento.
    -   Llame a la policía para obtener immediatamente una orden de protección.
    -   Lleve la orden consigo EN TODO MOMENTO, y dé copias a su familia, amistades, escuelas, empleadores y personas que cuidan a sus niños.

EN UNA EMERGENCIA—LLAME AL 911 DE INMEDIATO

INDEX

Tables and figures are indicated by an italic t and f following the page number

feminist theory, 19
Filipas, H. H., 107
Fine, M. A., 75
flexibility in group work, 33–34
follow-up groups, 10
food for childcare, 33t, 36–37
formal resources, seeking help through, 16
Frndak, K., 25

G

gender roles, changes in, 24
Genogram, 81, 86–87f, 90–91f
González-López, G., 24–25
graduation
    certificates, 123, 129f
    general discussion, 30t, 41, 123
    ongoing support after, 37
    overview, 6t
    suitcase activity, 124, 125–128f
group intervention model, 19
group theory, 25–26
group work
    assessment for domestic violence and safety planning, 35–36
    childcare, 36–37
    completion of program, ongoing support after, 37
    confidentiality and mandatory reporting, 36
    crisis interventions, 34–35
    cultural awareness, 28
    diversity in, 32–33
    dual role for facilitator and self-disclosure, 31
    flexibility in, 33–34
    format of, 32
    intake process, 35
    legal information, 36
    licensed mental health professionals as facilitators, 28
    mental health/domestic violence resource handout, 36
    physical environment, 32
    process and empowerment, 31–32
    reflection exercises, 29–30t
    roles and responsibilities for facilitators, 33t
    setting up groups, 32
    stages of, 5
    starting, 35–37
    teaching and instructional methods, 28–31
Guzmán, M. R., 81

H

Hartenberg, L., 11
healthy relationships
    background information on, 93–94
    Characteristics of Healthy Relationships handout, 93, 116, 155–156
    education on, 2
    general discussion, 93–94
    making changes, 2
    overview of topic, 6t, 29t, 40
    participants views on, 11
    review handout, 93, 100
    self-reflection writing and drawing activities, 95, 96–99f
    suggested readings, 94
    talking to children about, 116
help-seeking behaviors, 8, 16
    barriers to, 15–16
    familism and, 81
    intersectionality, 25
Hennepin County Legal Advocacy Project, 147
Hispanos en Minnesota, 147
Home Free Shelter, 147
homicidal ideation, 35
Hysjulien, B., 9

I

Identify problems/How do you cope? activity, 52, 53–54f, 57–58f
identity, 6t, 42
immigrant Latina women
    cultural concepts affecting perceptions of domestic violence, 8–9
    dating perspective, 75
    deportation, fear of, 16, 18, 36
    diversity in groups, 32–33
    educational groups for professionals working with, 3
    empowerment, 31–32
    general discussion, 1
    help-seeking behaviors among, 16
    immigration status, 17
    intake process, 35
    participation challenges, 4–5
    public benefits, access to, 17
    targeting in diverse social service agencies, 4
    transnational migrants, 17–18
immigrant status, 16, 17
Immigration and Nationality Act, 17
individual counseling, 37
informal resources, seeking help through, 16
INSIGHT program, 19
intake process, 33t, 34, 35
intersectionality, 24–25
interventions, 2, 19–20, 34–35
intimacy, 93
introductions, 39, 42
    general discussion, 42
    review handout, 49
    self-reflection drawing or writing activity, 44–48f
    suggested readings, 43